THE BIG BOOK STUDY

SPECIAL 2014 EDITION

Alcoholics Anonymous

In memory of all those whose lives ended while in
addiction, who never discovered this spiritual
path to recovery.

A Study of the Big Book of Alcoholic Anonymous

This book belongs to _____

CHAPTER 1

Introduction and History of the Big Book of Alcoholics Anonymous and the 12 Steps

For nearly 100 years God has used the healing power of the Big Book of Alcoholics Anonymous, the Twelve Steps and fellowship therein to restore the lives of countless individuals who suffer from a disease that centers in the mind, known as alcoholism, drug addiction, or any other lack of control-ism. He has conveyed this healing message through people who know what it is to be broken and restored by God. This book in print, eBook and audio is dedicated to all those who have found healing through this spiritual program and who continue to chose to share their experience, strength, and hope with those who are still seeking.

The history of the Twelve Step programs in Alcoholics Anonymous, Narcotics Anonymous and others can be traced back to the Oxford Group. The Oxford Group was an evangelistic movement from the early 1900's. A Lutheran minister by the name of Dr. Frank Buchman was the founder of the Oxford Group. Dr. Buchman experienced a spiritual transformation in 1908 as he visited a small church in Cumberland. He had a vision of the face of Jesus Christ and realized how his anger and resentments had separated himself from God's unconditional love. He surrendered his will to God and started to share his experience with others. The Bible says that when two or more people are gathered, that God is present in the Spirit. Dr. Buchman's work and following grew, and the fellowship groups eventually made it to Oxford, Princeton, Yale, Harvard, Williams, Smith and Vassar. The fellowship outreach was conducted through house meetings and members were encouraged to find and work with other people in their communities who suffered from problems similar to their own.

Bill Wilson, one of the co-founders of Alcoholics Anonymous, traced his journey to sobriety through the Oxford Group. An old friend of his Ebby Thatcher, was restored to sobriety through the Oxford Group. With his newfound sobriety he visited Bill Wilson and shared it with him. Bill Wilson took to the principles of the

Oxford Group and discovered his own personal transformation. He described his conversion experience from that night 20 years after the event in Alcoholics Anonymous Comes of Age: A Brief History of A.A., on page number 63: "My depression deepened unbearably and finally it seemed to me as though I were at the very bottom of the pit. I still gagged badly at the notion of a Power greater than myself, but finally, just for the moment, the last vestige of my proud obstinacy was crushed. All at once I found myself crying out, If there is a God, let Him show Himself! I am ready to do anything, anything!

Suddenly, the room lit up with a great white light. I was caught up into an ecstasy, which there are no words to describe. It seemed to me, in the mind's eye, that I was on a mountain and that a wind not of air but of spirit was blowing. And then it burst upon me that I was a free man. Slowly the ecstasy subsided. I lay on the bed, but now for a time I was in another world, a new world of consciousness. All about me and through me there was a wonderful feeling of Presence, and I thought to myself, 'So this is the God of the preachers! A great peace stole over me and I thought, No matter how wrong this seems to be, they are still all right. Things are all right with God and His world."

The development of Alcoholics Anonymous was underway, but Bill Wilson distanced himself from the Oxford Group in order to reach out to other groups who were uncomfortable with a religious, evangelical emphasis. Even so, most of the traditions of the Oxford Group continue in the A.A. approach and the Scriptures remain the foundation for recovery for many of those in A.A. and all the other Twelve Step programs.

More on the Oxford Group and its influence on AA

In the 1920's and 1930's, the Oxford Group movement became a revolutionary answer to antireligious reaction following World War 1. Striving to ignite a living faith in a church gone dry with institutionalism, the Oxford Group declared itself and "organism" rather than an "organization". To get back to activity, rather than rules and regulations, group members met in homes and hotels, mixing religion with meals. Despite its freedom from institutional ties, the movement still looked to the church as its authority and remained distinctly ecclesiastical.

Even considering that Dr. Frank Buchman, is most often cited as the leader of the Oxford movement, if you were to ask an Oxford Group follower, "Who is your leader?" the reply might be, "The Holy Spirit." The groups mantra was a belief in the guidance of the Spirit that it had no organized board of officers to get in the way, but relied instead on "God control" through men and women who had fully "surrendered" to God's will. It was Dr. Buchman who emphasized the need to fully surrender to God for forgiveness and guidance and to confess one's sins to God and to another person. Oxford Group followers also learned to make a living amends for wrongs they had done. They also believed that to witness to others who still suffered, about their changed lives, was a healing process.

The Oxford Group's teachings rested on the following six assumptions:

1)   Human beings are sinners.
2)   Human beings can be changed.
3)   Confession is a prerequisite to change.
4)   The changed soul has direct access to God.
5)   The age of miracles has returned.
6)   Those who have been changed are to change others.

Bill Wilson incorporated into AA's philosophy the Oxford Group's five procedures, which were:

1)   Giving to God.

2)   Listening to God's direction.
3)   Checking guidance.
4)   Restitution.
5)   Sharing, both confession and witness.

Both Wilson and Smith attended Oxford Group meetings and based much of the AA program on this framework. While trying to attract more followers to sobriety from 1935-1937, Smith and Wilson attended Oxford Group meetings in New York led by Samuel Shoemaker, Jr. "It was from Sam Shoemaker that we absorbed most of the Twelve Steps of Alcoholics Anonymous, steps that express the heart of AA's way of life," Wilson later said, "The early AA got its ideas of self-examination, acknowledgment of character defects, restitution for harm done, and working with others straight from the Oxford Group and directly from Sam Shoemaker, their former leader in America, and from nowhere else."

Now that we have some knowledge of our AA history, lets get to work. The primary purpose of this Study Guide is to understand The Big Book of Alcoholics Anonymous. The intention is to guide the reader based on experience and knowledge of alcoholism and the Program of Recovery. This guide can be used by an individual or by a group. This guide examines the content of the Big Book text.

Students and practitioners of the Big Book of AA rarely, if ever, return to drinking consistently. It has proved a solution of action to all our problems. Proof of this is the fact that a large number of other fellowships have borrowed and adapted the Twelve Steps and Twelve Traditions to find a solution to their particular problems which have nothing to do with drinking like: NA, Al-ANON, Overeaters Anonymous and others.

Faith is awesome and has to be attained, but faith has to be followed up by action. The Big Book of AA provides clear and concise directions on what we must do to have that faith.

In AA meetings we get to see miracle after miracle of newcomers find recovery. This builds our faith because we see it working in action.

Chapter 2

The Doctor's Opinion

The "Doctor's Opinion" was written by William D. Silkworth, MD. To a large percentage of people in recovery, this section of the Big Book is the most important. It describes alcoholism in a way that makes sense and resonates to the real alcoholic. From this concise description, the alcoholic learns the exact nature of the disease of alcoholism by marrying the obsession of the mind and the allergy of the body. The most important point the Doctor makes is that once we take that first drink we are unable to stop at just one or two. Our stop button no longer works.

He also expresses his belief, based on observations, that the Program of Alcoholics Anonymous is affective as a method of assuring the psychic change needed for what he believed to be the only solution for a seemingly hopeless state of mind and body.

Dr. Silkworth was a noted physician who was trained in neurology. He lost his practice after the 1929 stock market crash. He became involved in Townes Hospital which specialized in the treatment of alcoholics and drug addicts after meeting Charlie Townes. Dr. Silkworth took a position for a salary of $40.00 a week with plans to enter private practice again later. Instead, he devoted his entire career to a practice of helping alcoholics. The first waves of thousands upon thousands of alcoholics were directed to Alcoholics Anonymous, in part, because of his faith in our way of life.

Without Dr. William Silkworth, Alcoholics Anonymous wouldn't have happened as we know it. His opinion shaped the early foundation by clearly defining the problem so that a solution could be found. Proof of this is that Bill W understood the hopelessness of his alcoholism from Dr. Silkworth's opinion. Then, Dr. Bob understood the hopelessness of his alcoholism because Bill W explained Dr. Silkworth's opinion to him.

The Doctor's Opinion gives some necessary insight into the first step of AA, that if an alcoholic really wants to stop drinking for good, he must fully admit to his innermost self that he is powerless to a hopeless condition of mind, body and spirit. The first step in recovery and the "Doctor's Opinion" gives us the knowledge to surrender to that truth.

Questions on the Doctor's Opinion by William Silkworth

1. Do real alcoholics drink to escape?
2. What do many alcoholics try to do to stop drinking?
3. Is it easy to classify alcoholics?
4. How many types of alcoholic does Dr. Silkworth explore?
5. Identify type one?
6. Identify type two?
7. Identify type three?
8. Identify type four?
9. Identify type five?
10. Which one is the most common?
11. Are there any more types?
12. What do each type have in common?
13. What differentiates these alcoholic people apart from all other people?
14. What is the only proven relief from alcoholism?
15. Which treatment program has been successful in treating alcoholics?

1. What is the general consensus of physicians about alcoholics?
2. How does Dr. Silkworth demonstrate the solution to chronic alcoholism?
3. What was the solution to the first alcoholic's problem?
4. What was the solution to the second alcoholic's problem?
5. Which chapter did this alcoholic write in the Big Book? (Chapter 10 "To Employers."

1. What is the solution to the second man's alcoholism?
2. Did it work for him? How?
3. What does Dr. Silkworth advise every alcoholic to do?
4. If an alcoholic is led to carefully study the Big Book of AA, what might he end up doing?

1. What do we of Alcoholics Anonymous believe about this book?
2. What is the source of the convincing testimony in this particular book?
3. Who gave Alcoholics Anonymous this "opinion of alcoholism?
4. What was his position?
5. What was Dr. Silkworth specialize in?
6. How did Dr. Silkworth describe the patient Bill W. in 1934?
7. What happened during Bill's treatment?
8. In Bill's recovery, what did he try to impress upon other alcoholics?
9. His work was the basis for what?
10. How many did Dr. Silkworth say recovered by 1939?
11. Did Dr. Silkworth know some of them? How many?

In the original Big Book of AA, Dr. Silkworth said, "I personally know of 30 of these cases who were of the type with whom other methods had failed completely."

Dr. Silkworth put his reputation on the line for these 30 hopeless cases that he saw recover with Bill W. in Townes Hospital. The other 60 plus recovered alcoholics were in Akron or Cleveland.

Why are these facts of medical importance?

1. Did Dr. Silkworth believe this Program of recovery would work for many others?
2. Did Dr. Silkworth have confidence in recovered alcoholics? Explain?
3. What did the authors of this Book request of Dr. Silkworth?
4. What is Dr. Silkworth's largest statement?
5. What fact does Dr. Silkworth confirm suffering alcoholics must believe?
6. What issues didn't satisfy us?
7. Was there any truth in them?
8. Of what are we sure?
9. What must be included to make the picture of alcoholism a full one?
10. Which part of the doctor's theory is of interest to alcoholics?
11. Do we favor hospitalization for the very sick alcoholics?
12. What is usually necessary before we can begin to work with an alcoholic?

1. What was Dr. Silkworth's position?
2. What did his hospital specialize in?
3. Who should be interested in what is contained in this book?
4. What did Dr. Silkworth say that doctors believed important to alcoholics?
5. Did Dr. Silkworth believe the material in this book was of sufficient substance to warrant his contribution?
6. As much as the medical profession had going for them, what were the doctors not able or equipped to do?

7. Did Dr. Silkworth believe the medical profession had the ability to really help the alcoholic?

1. What was it that Bill W wanted to do with the ideas he had acquired?
2. What privilege did Bill W request of Dr. Silkworth?
3. Was Dr. Silkworth supportive of the idea?
4. How did he feel about the cases that he reviewed after Bill W did it?
5. How did Dr. Silkworth view recovered alcoholics?
6. What do recovered alcoholics believe?
7. On what page does Dr. Silkworth mention "moral psychology," followed by "powers of good" and finally "power".

1. What did Dr. Silkworth believe was the cause of the alcoholic's out-of-control drinking? (powerlessness)?
2. Does this "phenomenon" exist with normal drinkers?
3. How many drinks can a real alcoholic safely have?
4. Once the alcoholic has progressed into the "hopeless state", what transpires?
5. Can emotional pleading or reasoning help an alcoholic see the truth?
6. What type of message can help an alcoholic?
7. Who is best to carry the message to another alcoholic?
8. In what must an alcoholic's ideals be found in?
9. What would cause psychiatrists to accept and endorse/recommend the Program of AA?
10. What did Dr. Silkworth believe could do a more effective job in helping other alcoholics?
11. Why do alcoholics drink?
12. Does the alcoholic understand why he drinks?

13. Does drinking cause problems as Dr. Silkworth terms them?
14. What is the real problem with the alcoholic?
15. What is normal to the real alcoholic?
16. In the absence of a few drinks, what does the alcoholic feel?
17. What can they experience from taking a few drinks?

1. What effect do alcoholics see others experience when they drink?
2. What happens after the alcoholic gives in to that desire for a few drinks?
3. Does the alcoholic feel like he should be able to drink like other men?
4. What is the result of the first few drinks?
5. How does the alcoholic feel afterward?
6. Does that alcoholic seem to feel so remorseful that he challenges himself?
7. What is the resolution of every alcoholic?
8. How well does the real alcoholic keep the resolution to never take another drink?
9. Does it seem like the alcoholic is unmanageable?
10. To be successful in sobriety, what must the alcoholic experience?
11. Once an alcoholic has experienced an "entire psychic change," what happens next?
12. What happens next?
13. Does having a few simple rules "The Twelve Steps of AA" seem like a good idea?

1. What did the men who cried out to Dr. Silkworth plead for?
2. Do doctors, if they are honest with themselves, feel adequate in dealing with alcoholics?
3. What is "it" when a doctor gives all that is in him?

4. What can human power "not" do?
5. Can psychiatric efforts help a real alcoholic?
6. Have medicine and psychiatry made any progress in treating chronic alcoholism?
7. Did Dr. Silkworth believe that a real alcoholic could recover mental control to remedy his own problem with alcohol?
8. In his example, was the alcoholic having a bad time?
9. What insane act did he carry out?
10. Does this demonstrate "unmanageability"?
11. As a result of taking a drink, what happened next?
12. Does this demonstrate "powerlessness"?

Main Points of "The Doctor's Opinion"

1. The main point of Alcoholics Anonymous is to show precisely how and what specific actions, we have recovered.
2. Dr. Silkworth contends that the discoveries outlined in this book are of extraordinary medical importance and may represent a remedy for alcoholism.
3. The medical community has recognized but cannot provide a remedy based on "moral psychology".
4. Alcoholism is a "hopeless" "Illness" as there is no effective treatment, medicine or scientific remedy.
5. Alcoholics need some "power" greater than themselves to recover.
6. Dr. Silkworth describes loss of control and craving as central symptoms of alcoholism.
7. To produce the central psychic change needed to cure alcoholism something more than human power is needed.

Chapter 3

Bill's Story

In the "Doctor's Opinion" we learned the exact nature of the disease of alcoholism. We learned that we are powerless because of the allergic reaction the alcoholic has to alcohol manifests in the craving that comes with the first few drinks. We learned of the unmanageability resulting from a mind that cannot remember the allergic reaction and began to start drinking again as if "this time" we can control it.

The main purpose of Bill's Story is for identification. In "Bill's Story" we will essentially be "12th Stepped" by Bill W himself. We will see the progression of the disease in his life. While studying his story, it is important to look for the effect of drinking on that you have also experienced. Find and key in on the similarities and discard the differences. We can look at what happened to him and say, "Yup that happened to me as well."

In sobriety meetings we have a saying, "If it fits, let it stick."

We learn how Bill first found some hope after meeting his long time friend Ebby Thatcher. Ebby became Bill's sponsor while Bill was in the hospital in Townes. Ebby continued to visit Bill and helped him get into action through the Twelve Steps. During this process Bill had a spiritual experience. Bill goes on to tell us in his story what he got out of 36 years of action through the program, by not taking a drink, one day at a time.

1. Where was Bill when he first drank?
2. What happened with these officers?
3. What did he find in these homes?
4. What was his mood like?
5. What did he forget?
6. What was his mood like when he started drinking again?
7. Did Bill drink to change how he thought and felt? Due to loneliness?
8. When Bill visited Winchester Cathedral, what caught his attention?
9. How did it affect him?
10. How old was Bill at the end of the war?
11. Did Bill seem to think well of himself?
12. What gave him that idea?
13. Were his ideas pretty large?

1. Was Bill willing to do the work to be successful?
2. What did he want to prove?
3. What did he become interested in?
4. What did Bill study, besides law?
5. Did his drinking help his education?
6. How did his wife feel about his drinking?
7. What did he tell his wife Lois?
8. Although he studied law, what really interested him?
9. Who were Bill's heroes?

10. What did alcohol and speculation do for Bill?
11. Were Bill's broker friends willing to help him?
12. Did Bill have a strong will?
13. What was Bill's theory?
14. What did Bill and his wife do that seemed crazy?
15. How did they do it?
16. What did their friends think of the idea?

1. How long did they stick with the motorcycle?
2. Was their investigation of companies on the East Coast productive?
3. How were their finances at the end of the year?
4. Did this adventure lead to success for Bill?
5. Were people impressed with Bill's judgment?
6. What period of time does this cover?
7. How did drinking fit into Bill's life?
8. Was Bill a social guy? Was he successful in making friends?
9. How often did Bill drink?
10. What did Bill's friends think of his drinking?
11. How was Bill's relationship with Lois going?
12. Was Bill faithful?
13. Did Bill want to be a professional athlete? What sport?
14. Was he better at his sport or at drinking?
15. How did Bill feel in the morning?

1. Was Bill successful financially?
2. Did it seem like Bill had the ability to be successful?
3. What transpired in 1929?
4. Did it have a big impact on Bill?
5. What are some of the worst examples of other people's reactions to their losses?
6. How did Bill look at what others were doing?
7. What was Bill's solution to his losses?
8. What was his attitude about it?

9. Did his drinking change the way he thought and felt?
10. Where did Bill go after for another chance?
11. Who was it he felt like?
12. What was his second failure after the stock market crash (Black Friday)
13. Where did he and Lois go next?
14. How did he lose his job?
15. How long did he go without a job?
16. How was his drinking progressing?
17. Who took care of the finances?
18. What was Lois's life like after a hard day of work?

1. Were Bill's business associates happy to see him?
2. How did alcohol change Bill?
3. What was Bill drinking and how?
4. How did Bill start waking up?
5. What did Bill have to do?
6. Did Bill think he had a problem with drinking yet?
7. What gave Lois hope?
8. Did things get better for Bill?
9. Did Bill get another chance in business?
10. What kind of deal did Bill put together?
11. What was Bill's motivation for this deal?
12. Why wasn't it successful?
13. Because of this episode, what did Bill learn?
14. What had Bill done before this time?
15. Was Bill absolutely serious this time?
16. How well did Bill do with his decision?
17. Did he make a conscious decision to have a drink?
18. What did his shocking lack of perspective make him wonder?
19. What was his next decision/understanding?

1. What happened to Bill when he got confident?
2. Why did Bill enter the café?
3. Was he conscious of having the first drink?
4. What did Bill tell himself after he felt the effect of the whisky in the milk?
5. How did Bill feel the next morning?
6. Did Bill feel defeated?
7. What was Bill's thinking process like?
8. Was Bill afraid to cross the street?
9. What did it take to calm his nerves?
10. What did Bill realize when he learned of another stock market crash?
11. What did Bill consider doing?
12. What did Bill do to quiet his thinking?
13. How much longer did Bill struggle with alcoholism?
14. Did Bill steal to drink?
15. Did Bill think about killing himself?
16. Did Bill go from place to place hoping?
17. Did Bill fear for his life?
18. What did Bill do with his mattress and why?
19. What did the doctor do for Bill?

1. What was Bill doing the next day?
2. What did they do for Bill?
3. What was the concern for Bill?
4. Had Bill's drinking progressed to where he couldn't eat?
5. Did Bill seem to be dying at this point?
6. What did his brother in law and mother do?
7. What treatments did they give Bill?
8. What happened to Bill in the hospital?
9. What did the Doctor explain to Bill?
10. Did it seem to make sense to Bill and relieve him?
11. Did the good Doctor help Bill understand why he couldn't stop drinking?
12. When Bill believed that he now understood his problem, how did he feel?

13. How long did this help him stay sober?
14. What was he able to do?
15. Once we know what is wrong with us are we always able to stop drinking?
16. How well did self knowledge work for Bill?
17. Was Bill's judgment and health falling apart fast?
18. What did Bill do now?
19. What did Bill think this trip was?
20. What did Lois learn from Dr. Silkworth?
21. What did Dr. Silkworth tell Lois her two options were?
22. Did they have to tell Bill?
23. Was Bill looking forward to dying?
24. What did this do to Bill's self worth?

1. Did Bill prove that he could make things happen in his life?
2. Could he discern where he was headed?
3. Who did Bill think about?
4. What did he really want to do?
5. Did he have any hope left?
6. What did Bill feel? (This is where Bill took Step One)
7. What did Bill completely surrender to?
8. How did Bill leave the hospital the second time?
9. What kept Bill from taking the first drink?
10. What caused Bill to start drinking again? (Does this seem like insanity?)
11. When did it fail him?
12. What was everyone's thoughts about Bill's situation?
13. What was this last drinking binge to be for Bill?
14. What was to become of Bill?
15. What was it Bill would come to know?
16. What was Bill doing around the end of November of 1934?
17. What caused the feeling of satisfaction Bill was experiencing?
18. Where was Bill thinking of hiding a bottle?

19. Why did he feel it was needed to have a bottle under his bed?
20. What interrupted Bill's daydreaming?
21. Whose voice did Bill hear?
22. What did Ebby want to do?

1. What condition was Ebby in?
2. How did this affect Bill?
3. What rumor about Ebby had Bill heard?
4. What did Bill imagine?
5. What were Bill's plans?
6. When bill saw Ebby at the door, what did Bill see?
7. What did Bill think?
8. What did Bill do?
9. What did Ebby do?
10. How did this effect Bill?
11. What did Bill ask Ebby?
12. What was Ebby's answer? How did he give Bill the answer?
13. How did Bill react?
14. What did Bill suspect of his old friend?
15. What did Bill notice about Ebby?
16. What did Bill decide?
17. Why didn't he mind if Ebby wanted to do some preaching?
18. What did Ebby tell Bill?
19. What had these two men told Ebby?
20. How long had Ebby been sober?
21. What did Ebby's 2 months show Bill?
22. Why had Ebby called on Bill?

1. Was Bill really interested in what Ebby had to say?
2. Why was Bill so interested?
3. What did Ebby say to Bill?
4. Did what Ebby shared impact Bill?

5. How is the word denial used in this paragraph?
6. Besides Bill's childhood, what else did Ebby remind Bill of?
7. What had Bill always believed?
8. Was Bill an atheist? An agnostic?
9. What did Bill believe?
10. What did he ask himself?
11. Where did Bill draw the line concerning religions?
12. What was Bill's attitude when someone wanted to pray or talk to God?
13. What was Bill's attitude about Jesus Christ?
14. How did Bill feel about Jesus's teachings?
15. Was Bill a Christian?
16. What made Bill skeptical?
17. What was Bill's attitude about organized religion?
18. From what Bill had witnessed, he believed what?
19. Who did Bill believe was the boss of the universe?
20. What did Ebby declare to Bill?
21. How did Ebby's willpower help Bill?
22. What hope had the doctor's given Ebby?
23. What happened because of this for Bill?
24. What had they both done?
25. What happened to Ebby?
26. Did Ebby accomplish this miracle by his own power?
27. Did Ebby share the same powerlessness that Bill experienced?
28. How did that affect Bill?
29. What did it look like to Bill?
30. What started to happen to Bill's ideas?
31. What did Ebby appear to be to Bill at that moment?
32. What did that tell Bill?
33. What did Bill see in Ebby?

1. Did Bill see a authentic difference in Ebby?

2. How did seeing this miracle change Bill's outlook on God?
3. What word did Bill dislike?
4. How did the idea of a personal God affect Bill?
5. Did Bill still hold on to agnostic views?
6. Did Bill find other people who shared his views of God?
7. When Ebby realized Bill's issue, what did he suggest to Bill?
8. How did that suggestion work with Bill?
9. What happened?
10. Bill then stood where?
11. What must we be willing to believe?
12. Can we come to believe in a power greater than ourselves?
13. What more is needed to make a new beginning?
14. When does spiritual growth start?
15. What is the foundation of success in the Program of AA?
16. Did Bill decide he would have it?
17. What was Bill convinced of now?
18. What was Bill now able to do?
19. What fell from his eyes?
20. What was he now able to see?
21. Is this Step Two?
22. What did Bill realize about the "doggerel on the old tombstone" at Winchester Cathedral?
23. For a moment, Bill had needed and wanted what?
24. When Bill was willing to call on God, what happened?
25. What ended Bill's feeling of the presence of God?

1. How long and what kept Bill from being able to sense that presence again?
2. What happened at Townes Hospital?
3. Why did Bill go to Townes Hospital?
4. When did Bill enter the hospital?

5. What was the first thing he reported at the hospital?
6. Is this Step 3?
7. What did he do related to Step 6 and Step 7?
8. Was he willing to face things and become willing?
9. When did Bill make this decision?
10. Was taking these action steps a positive for Bill's sobriety?
11. What did Bill share with Ebby?
12. What list did Bill make with Ebby's help?
13. What Steps are they related to?
14. Did Bill intend to make amends/restitution?
15. What Step is this?
16. What did Bill do to test his drinking?
17. What Step is this?
18. What did Ebby tell Bill would happen to his thinking?
19. What was Bill to do when in doubt?
20. What did Ebby tell Bill related to how often he could pray for himself?
21. Did Ebby tell Bll that prayer and meditation would be good?
22. How did she tell him?
23. Ebby promised Bill that once he had taken the Steps, Bill would know what two things?
24. What did Ebby tell Bill were the essential requirements for real success in sobriety?

PAGE 14

1. Is the program simple?
2. Is the program easy?
3. Is this precious thing a gift?
4. What must be destroyed?
5. Do I have to let go of handling every element of my life?

6. Who do I have to hand over control of my life to?
7. Were these common proposals?
8. What happened to Bill once he accepted them?
9. How does Bill describe his spiritual experience?
10. After it passed, what was Bill's concern?
11. Did Dr. Silkworth really listen to Bill?
12. What did the doctor say?
13. Was Bill's spiritual experience the only one Dr. Silkworth witnessed?
14. What was Dr. Silkworth's view on spiritual experiences?
15. What thought came to Bill while he was in the hospital?
16. What did Ebby tell Bill was mandatory?
17. What was particularly important?
18. What did Ebby say must be added to faith?
19. Is this especially true for alcoholics?
20. How does an alcoholic develop his spiritual life?
21. Why is it so important for an alcoholic to help others?
22. If an alcoholic in recovery doesn't work with others, what will happen?
23. Where would our faith be then?
24. What did Bill and Lois do?
25. Did it interfere with Bill's business activities?
26. How long did Bill go without work?
27. What was Bill plagued with?
28. What almost drove Bill to drink?
29. What solution did Bill find?
30. What did Bill do many times?
31. How was he feeling when he went?
32. What happened when he talked to another alcoholic?
33. What is the Program of Alcoholics Anonymous about?
34. What did Bill and Lois find happening to them?
35. What did they find to be true under duress?
36. What did they see happening to families?
37. What happened to some who came from asylums?

38. What happened to business and professional people?
39. What form of trouble and misery isn't overcome when we practice the AA Program?
40. Why did they have meetings?
41. What is an alcoholic who is drinking?
42. How did Bill describe our struggles with the wet ones?
43. What did one alcoholic do in Bill and Lois's home?
44. Why?
45. What is it we have?
46. Are some people shocked at our attitude?
47. What underlies our purpose?
48. What must work in and through us?
49. How long must it work?
50. If we don't live by faith, what will happen to us?
51. What do most of us feel?
52. When do we experience the real blessings of the Program of AA?

MAIN POINTS TO BILL'S STORY

1. Alcoholism is a hopeless illness that is marked by loss of control and obsession with the first drink.
2. The power of one alcoholic talking to another alcoholic
3. The insanity of the first drink is beyond human aid.
4. The solution for the real alcoholic is spiritual.
5. Carl Jung and William James support the spiritual experience.

Chapter 4

There is a Solution

Summary

In THERE IS A SOLUTION, we find the ansnwers to that seemingly hopeless state of mind and body. We will learn where this solution came from and the concise directions for taking the actions that it takes to be assured that we are able to join that first 100 recovered alcoholics.

The difference between the fellowship and the program will be revealed. Even though we face a common problem, knowing this alone, isn't the solution. We have to learn the very real truths about the disease of alcoholism. We learn about the Dr. Jeckyl and Mr. Hyde style of addiction. We learn that the physical allergy to alcohol isn't what drives us to AA for help. The real problem centers in the mind.

We learn that the main problem for the alcoholic isn't drinking. Alcoholics can drink well, better than the rest. We learn that stopping isn't the problem either. All of us have stopped a bunch of times. We just can't stay stopped. Our stop button is eternally broken and the shop can't fix it. The real problem for every real alcoholic is that we can't stop for good. The real alcoholic mind doesn't have the ability to manage the decision to stay stopped; that produces the "insidious insanity" that leads to the first drink. The lack of the ability to stop on our own makes it necessary to build a relationship with God (Higher Power) to remove the need to try to manage a decision to never drink again.

In "There is a Solution" we also learn about 3 types of drinkers. 1) Moderate drinkers. 2) Hard drinkers who can drink moderately or stop altogether if they choose. 3) The real alcoholic who is totally powerless over alcohol. Those of us in this category come to find out that Alcoholics Anonymous is our ticket to recovery. Through the Twelve Steps and Twelve Traditions we learn how to live life on life's terms.

ADD PAGE NUMBERS AND NOTES

1. What do we know?
2. What have they done?
3. Who are members of Alcoholics Anonymous?
4. Would we have known each other without AA?
5. What do alcoholics share?
6. Does Alcohol affect all races, creeds, religions?
7. Are rich people exempt from alcoholism?
8. Who are we like?
9. How are we unlike them?
10. What feeling have we all shared?
11. Will the common problem keep us together?
12. What fact does keep us together?
13. What can we agree on?
14. We can join in what?

15. Is the effect of our disease limited to just the alcoholic?
16. What are our feeling to a cancer patient?
17. What goes with alcoholism?
18. Who does it affect?
19. What does it bring to all those affected by alcoholism?
20. What is our hope?
21. Is this for just a few?
22. Are we willing to talk about our issues with professionals or even our family and friends?
23. What can the recovered alcoholic do?
24. When can some growth be made with the suffering alcoholic?
25. What is it that the recovering alcoholic brings to the suffering alcoholic?
26. Can someone with just a little bit of sober time help someone else?

1. What happens after the recovered alcoholic tells his story to someone still suffering?
2. How many of us earn our living 12th stepping alcoholics?
3. What is the elimination of drinking?
4. What is more important than not drinking?
5. How many of the authors worked with suffering alcoholics?
6. What are some of the fortunate able to do?
7. Will AA end alcoholism?
8. In large cities like Dallas what are we overcome by?
9. Many alcoholics could recover if what?
10. What question faced the first hundred?
11. What conclusion did the first one hundred come to?
12. What is the content of the Big Book?
13. Who could benefit from this experience and knowledge?
14. What will it be necessary to discuss?

15. The authors were aware of what?
16. What would really please the authors?
17. What did the authors of this book strive to achieve?
18. What do most of us sense?
19. What is it that our lives depend on?
20. What may you have already asked?
21. What are you probably curious about?
22. If you are an alcoholic who wants recovery, what are you asking?
23. What is the purpose of this book?
24. What will the first one hundred tell us in this book?
25. Before answering these questions, what did the authors do?
26. What have people said to the suffering alcoholic many times?
27. Are these commonplace observations?
28. What is behind them?
29. Do these comments come from alcoholics?
30. What is a moderate drinker?
31. What can they do that alcoholics can't?
32. What is the next type of drinker?
33. Could his habit become serious?

1. What could it do to him?
2. Can the hard drinker stop or moderate if given a good reason?
3. Could he benefit from treatment?
4. Do the hard drinker and real alcoholic look similar?
5. What is the big difference between the hard drinker and the real alcoholic?
6. What is especially puzzling about the real alcoholic?
7. What does he do while drinking?
8. Does the real alcoholic have a change of personality when drinking?
9. Is the real alcoholic usually only buzzed?

10. He is almost always in what condition?
11. Are real alcoholics decent people when sober?
12. What happens when they drink?
13. At what is he a genius?
14. Is the real alcoholic a normal person in every other way?
15. What is that one way?
16. In this one respect, they are incredibly what?
17. Are most alcoholics talented and capable?
18. How does the real alcoholic use his gifts?
19. What does the alcoholic do to have success?
20. Should a drunk alcoholic sleep all day and all night?
21. What is the alcoholics sleep interrupted for?
22. If an alcoholic has enough money, what does he do?
23. Why would he do that?
24. When alcohol quits working, what do many alcoholics add to their drinking?
25. What do they hope to accomplish?
26. What follows this effort?
27. What is the next step to continue to be able to function?
28. Then where do real alcoholics wind up?
29. Is the foregoing a complete picture of the real alcoholic?
30. Does it come close?
31. If hundreds of drunk experiences end in catastrophe, what are the questions?
32. Do we have some understanding of this today?
33. Can we answer the riddle?
34. Of what are we certain?
35. Of what are we equally positive?
36. Does the ingestion of alcohol affect both the body and the mind?
37. What is the result of taking any alcohol into the body of an alcoholic?

1. What makes the preceding statement exceedingly clear?
2. What sets the cycle in motion?
3. Where does the real problem of the real alcoholic lay?
4. If you ask an alcoholic why he drinks, can he give you an honest answer?
5. What analogy do the authors give us?
6. If you point this out to him, what will be his reaction?
7. Does the alcoholic ever tell the truth?
8. What is the truth?
9. Do they know the answer?
10. What is the real truth?
11. Once they have crossed the line what is their mental state?
12. What is the obsession of every alcoholic?
13. Do they get caught up on trying over and over again to prove they can drink like a gentleman if they just try harder?
14. Do they normally suspect the truth, that they can't stop?
15. What do family members and friends hope?
16. What is the tragic truth?
17. What has the alcoholic lost?
18. What happens at a certain point in the alcoholics drinking career?
19. What is the tragic situation?
20. What is it that the alcoholic lost?
21. What happens to our willpower?
22. How long can we rely on our minds to keep the misery of our last drunk remembered?
23. As a result of this forgetter phenomenon, what are we without?
24. With no more than one drink, what does not enter our mind?
25. If there is any suspicion, what does the mind do?
26. What analogy do they give us regarding the loss of the power of choice?

27. What does the alcoholic say to himself?
28. Do alcoholics always give some thought to taking that first drink?
29. Does it seem like some alcoholics drink before realizing what they are doing?
30. When they realize they are drinking, what thoughts do they have?
31. When an alcoholic reaches this stage of alcoholism, where do they find themselves?
32. If not locked up, what will happen to them?
33. Do you believe this is fact or fiction?

1. What has prevented many such demonstrations?
2. What are so many unable to do?
3. Is there a solution?
4. Does the alcoholic like the solution?
5. What do they not like?
6. Are these necessary actions to have success in sobriety?
7. What gave us hope?
8. What were we faced with when confronted by recovered alcoholics?
9. For those of us who have adopted spiritual principles, what have we experienced?
10. What is the great fact for us?
11. What is the central fact in our lives today?
12. What has He commenced in doing?
13. Is there a middle of the road solution for real alcoholics?
14. How were our lives?
15. What were the two alternatives?

Appendix ll Third page 569 & Fourth page 567

16. Upon careful reading, what do we learn is the product of a "spiritual experience" and a "spiritual awakening"?
17. What impression did the readers of the First Printing of the First Edition get?

18. This conclusion is what?
19. In the stories in the first chapters, which spiritual event was described?
20. Did most alcoholics believe they, too, must have a spiritual experience?
21. Are such transformations frequent?
22. What do most of our member's experience?
23. Why did William James call them that?
24. Who are the first to notice the change that has taken place?
25. What does the alcoholic finally realize?
26. Could he have accomplished this himself?
27. What could seldom have been accomplished by self discipline?
28. With few exceptions, what do we all tap into?

1. What do they identify this to be?
2. What do most of us think?
3. What do religious folks call it?
4. What do we wish to say emphatically to any alcoholic?
5. What is one condition the alcoholic must meet?
6. What will defeat an alcoholic?
7. What is it that no one should have difficulty with?
8. What are the essentials of recovery?
9. How important are they?
10. What will keep a person in everlasting ignorance?

PAGE 26

1. Why did they accept spiritual help?
2. Talk about and describe Rowland H?
3. Where did he seek help?

4. Who did he go to?
5. Was he confident that he had been fixed?
6. How were his physical and mental conditions after treatement?
7. Above all, what did he believe?
8. What happened?
9. How did he explain it?
10. What did he do?
11. Did he respect the doctor?
12. What did he ask of the doctor?
13. What was his greatest wish?
14. Was he a normal person?
15. What was it he didn't have control over?
16. What was his first question?
17. What did he want to know?
18. What was the truth?
19. What did he have to do to live?
20. Who told him?
21. Did he die from drinking?
22. Did he need to be protected from himself?
23. Was he free to come and go?
24. What do he have to do to maintain his freedom from alcohol?
25. Do some think they can do it without help? Without spiritual help?
26. What do the authors tell us?
27. What did the doctor tell Rowland his problem was?
28. How many alcoholics had Dr. Jung seen recover?
29. How did Rowland react to his prognosis?
30. What did he ask the doctor?
31. What did the doctor say?
32. Were there exceptions?
33. How common?
34. Did Dr. Jung understand these occurrences?
35. What did these important spiritual experiences appear to be to Dr. Jung?
36. What was the sum of these occurrences?
37. What had Dr. Jung been attempting to do with Rowland?

38. Had Dr. Jung been successful with hard drinkers?
39. Had he had any success with a real alcoholic?
40. Was Rowland relieved to hear the Dr.'s solution?
41. Why did he have hope?
42. What did Dr. Jung do to Rowland's hope?
43. What made Rowland a free man?
44. What does the Program of AA give the suffering alcoholic?
45. What is another way to view what we are given?
46. What contribution did William James make to AA?
47. What do we not want to do?
48. What does the experience of the first 100 mean?
49. When will this happen?
50. Will the Program of AA as described in the Big Book, disturb any religious views?
51. Do we care what religious groups our members belong to?
52. Do we define who God is or isn't?
53. How do we view that topic?
54. Do all of us join a religious group?
55. Do some of us join a religious group?
56. Do we favor such association?
57. What will we learn in the next chapter?
58. What is the chapter after that one about?
59. Do we get a lot of agnostics in AA?
60. Is being agnostic a handicap to recovery?
61. What is the biggest problem for those who already believe in God, as they understand Him, in recovery. Hint (Faith)
62. What comes after the Basic Text of the Big Book?
63. What does each individual do by telling his story?
64. Do they talk about their experience, strength and hope?
65. What do the stories accomplish?
66. What do we hope those who read the stories will not do?
67. What do we hope the stories will do for the suffering alcoholic?

Main Points

1. The telling of one's story as a case presentation.
2. The importance of the consequent "hopelessness" or "emotional bottom".
3. The delivery of the message of recovery by one alcoholic helping another.
4. The importance of a spiritual experience that leads to recovery.
5. The difference between "insanity" and an "spiritual experience".

CHAPTER 5

MORE ABOUT ALCOHOLISM

More About Alcoholism tells us that all alcoholics have one great obsession: to gain control over their drinking. Drug addicts, overeating, gambling and other compulsions battle the same mental gymnastics.

"Normal" drinkers have no problem controlling their drinking. If they do have a problem with drugs or alcohol, they simply adjust their use, and the problem goes away.

We're not so lucky. Control remains elusive. The recurring problems prevent us from really enjoying our use. But we press on, determined that one day, we'll be in charge and have a good time. We become obsessed by the idea. That in itself shows how important drinking and drugging has become in our lives. Not really normal, is it?

Our obsession makes it tough to admit that "someday" will never come for us. But that's the first step on the road to recovery. This chapter tells us that we must fully admit we're alcoholics. We must come clean with ourselves and fess up that we fit the definition of an alcoholic: we can't control our drinking and drugging. Somewhere along the way, we lost that ability.

Once we've lost that ability, nothing will bring it back. Doctors agree. Sixty years after the Big Book was written, science still hasn't found a way for addicts to regain control of their drugging. That's the simple truth about us.

Chances are, if you're one of us, you read those words and think, *Not me, I'm different. I'll prove them wrong.* Well, good luck. We tried all of the ways listed in chapter 3 and then some but found we couldn't do it.

This chapter calls alcoholism a "progressive illness." This means it gets worse with time, never better. Not even prolonged periods of abstinence will turn back its progression. Once it strikes us, addiction carries us along like a raft caught in the rapids.
Our obsession that someday we'll control and enjoy our drugging is an illusion. Not even thirty years of abstinence will change our situation. It's best to abandon the obsession.

Still not convinced? There's another test: stay clean and sober for a year. Few true alcoholics or addicts can. Fail the test, and that's another way to prove you're one of us. Catch is, even if you make it a year without any alcohol or drugs, you still haven't proven you're not an alcoholic or addict. Remember the guy sober thirty years. Once he started drinking again, he was dead in four. Can you say, "progressive illness"?

Chapter 3 of the Big Book talks about young people. Even those who hadn't been drinking long still found themselves as helpless as those who had been drinking twenty years. Addiction can happen quickly. Research has proven that the younger you are when you start drinking, the more likely you are to become addicted.

The Big Book tells us that 20 percent of AA's members are under thirty. We who are young are by no means safe from the grips of addiction. The good news is that we're also eligible to share in the solution.

So, why, despite past problems, do we addicts use again? In a word, *insanity*.

The insanity occurs in the way we twist our thinking to justify the decision to drink or use, despite overwhelming evidence that our decision is flawed. Such thinking usually precedes a relapse. We don't slip back into our addiction by any sane means.

Chapter 3 reminds us that this twisted thinking-this insanity-is common among addicts. Remember, we're obsessed with the idea that somehow, someday we'll control and enjoy our drinking and drugging. That obsession can drive us crazy.

This chapter talks about the insanity of jaywalking (crossing an intersection carelessly, such as when the light is red). Or driving the wrong way down a one-way street. It would be insane to keep driving into a lane of oncoming traffic. Well, that's how our drinking and drugging looks to others. Problem is, the ears are often the first to go. We can't hear their concerns because we're consumed by our obsession.

Some people who have had problems with drugs and

alcohol can change their use. Maybe you've seen this with your classmates or other using buddies. They had consequences and cut back or quit altogether. Problem solved. But the true addict isn't so lucky.

The authors say they want to smash home this point: You can't do it by yourself. Maybe you've tried. You know. If you're one of us and honest with yourself, you'll see what they say is true.

We meet Fred in chapter 3. He was a "not me" guy. He was confident that the problems others described couldn't happen to him. *Not me*. That state of mind can kill us. Further, if experience has shown otherwise-that we suffer the symptoms outlined here-then that state of mind is another form of insanity.

Underlying this "not me" mentality is the thought that somehow we're different from others. Those things may happen to them, but they won't happen to me. It's like believing you'll never be in a car accident. That always happens to other people, not me. It's a sort of ignorant arrogance.

Back to Fred, he drinks impulsively, with almost no thought, other than that a few drinks seem like a good idea. Bam! He's disappeared on a binge. That quick sleight of mind was all it took.

To Fred's credit, the experience taught him he had an "alcoholic mind," one prone to insanity. One prone to that flawed reasoning described earlier. One not to be trusted by itself. As AA members like to say, "My mind is like a bad neighborhood-I shouldn't go in there alone."

When Fred tells his two friends from AA how his mind tricked him, they grin. Not to laugh at him, but in recognition. They know that way of thinking-it was once their own. "Such an alcoholic mentality is a hopeless condition," they tell him.

They remind him there is a solution. They outline the spiritual remedy and "program of action." Like those before him, Fred isn't happy to learn that this "program of action" requires him to change his thinking and attitude. Yet, also like those others, his story has a happy ending. By the end of the chapter, his life has become more satisfying and useful to others.

The chapter concludes with a summary supported by the physician's opinion: Given their insane mentality, addicts are defenseless against drugs. Only a Higher Power can save them from their own thinking. Therein lies the solution.

1. What are most alcoholics unwilling to concede/admit?
2. What would nobody like to think?
3. What do our drinking careers demonstrate?
4. What is the great obsession of every alcoholic?
5. What is astonishing in the life of an alcoholic?
6. Where does the obsession/illusion take many of us?
7. Do most untreated alcoholics end up dying or in jail or in a mental institution?
8. What did we learn that is absolutely necessary for success?
9. Why is this so important?
10. Like the obsession/illusion, what must be happened to the delusion? (smashed)
11. What is the alcoholics problem?
12. What do we know?
13. What have all of us believed on occasion?
14. Where did this lead us?
15. Of what are we convinced?
16. Will it get better?
17. Who are we compared to?
18. Why?
19. How many remedies have we tried?
20. Have some of us found recovery?

21. What always followed this newfound hope?
22. On what do physicians agree?
23. Has science been able to fix us?
24. What do we try to prove and how do we try to prove it?
25. What will we do to the alcoholic who learns how to drink responsibly? (Hat)
26. What does heaven know?
27. What do alcoholics do to try to control their drinking?
28. Did all the things mention cover all of your own ideas?
29. What do we not like to do?
30. But what can a person do?
31. What is the first test suggested to try?
32. What do they mean by controlled drinking?
33. How many times does it say to try the test?
34. How soon will the real alcoholic know he/she is one of us?
35. What price may be paid to learn the truth?
36. What do most alcoholics believe?
37. Are some people successful by their own willpower?
38. What 6 important facts can be learned in the story of the "man of thirty"?
39. What kind of drinker was he?
40. What condition was he in the morning?
41. What did he do to take care of that condition?
42. What was his goal?
43. What was defeating him?
44. Why?
45. What did he decide he wanted to do?
46. What did he decide not to do?
47. What kind of man was he?
48. Why was he so exceptional?
49. Did 25 years of sobriety pay off?
50. Once retired what did he believe?
51. What did he do?
52. After 2 months of drinking, had his drinking problem progressed?
53. Did he try to control his drinking?

54. How?
55. Was he successful?
56. What measures did he try?
57. Did he try what he tried at age 30?
58. How did he do?

PAGE 33

1. How many attempts were successful?
2. Was he in good condition at age 55?
3. What did he do to stop drinking for good?
4. Are there lessons in this story?
5. What did he find when he started drinking again?
6. If we can stay sober for a while, will it be better if we drink again?
7. Are young people inclined to believe what he did when he was 30?
8. What did several young men discover?
9. Does how long a person drinks have anything to do with the disease?
10. Does a person have to drink long and hard to become a hopeless alcoholic?
11. Does alcoholism treat women differently? How about Black people or poor people?
12. What can be said for potential female alcoholics?
13. What are certain drinkers astonished to learn?
14. As we look back, what do we believe? (Page 34)
15. What is the second test to learn the truth about alcoholism?
16. Will real alcoholics be successful?
17. Can we be successful in the early stages of the disease?
18. What happens later on?
19. If a person fails the tests, will he be interested in the content of this book?
20. Even though a real alcoholic may decide to quit for a year, how soon will most return to drinking?

21. If a person can't drink moderately, what is the question?
22. What are we assuming?
23. What will determine whether a person can quit?
24. What do many of us feel we have?
25. What was our tremendous urge?
26. How successful were we?
27. What is the baffling feature of alcoholism?
28. No matter what?
29. What is the question at this point?
30. What will be helpful?
31. What will we describe?
32. Why describe this mental condition?
33. What is the question at this point? (Page 30)
34. What kind of family did Jim have?
35. What had he inherited?
36. How was his war record?
37. Was he good at his profession?
38. Was he likeable?
39. Was he dumb?
40. Was he normal?
41. Except for what?
42. When did he began drinking?
43. What happened after he left the mental institution?
44. What 2 things did the AA's tell him?
45. What did he do?
46. What happened as a result?
47. What did he not do?
48. How many times did he get drunk?
49. How many times did the recovered alcoholics see him?
50. What did the AA's do?
51. On what did he agree with them on?
52. What did he know would happen if he drank again?
53. What else did he know would happen?
54. What did he do anyway?
55. What did the AA's do?
56. How was Jim on Tuesday morning?
57. What was the source of his irritation?

58. Did he speak to his boss?
59. What did he decide to do?
60. Along the way what happened?
61. So, what did he do?
62. Did he stop for a drink?
63. What did he think he would do?
64. What else did he hope he might find?
65. Was this place unfamiliar with him?
66. Was it a set up to stop there?
67. What did he do after sitting down?
68. Had the thought of drinking entered his mind?
69. He was still hungry, what did he do?
70. What insane thought came to him?
71. Did he act sanely to the insane thought?
72. What did he sense?
73. What thought proceeded his decision to take the first drink?
74. What did he do?
75. Then what did he do?
76. Where did those 3 drinks take him?
77. What was placed at risk due to taking the drinks?
78. Did he know he was an alcoholic?
79. What happened to all his reasons for not taking the first drink?

PAGE 37

1. What would we call this action?
2. Is this an extreme case?
3. Is this farfetched to us?
4. Have some of us given more thought to the consequences than Jim did?
5. What is curious about the alcoholics thinking?
6. What overrode sound reasoning?
7. Will sound reasoning keep us safe from the first drink?
8. What always wins out?

9. What do we then earnestly and sincerely ask?
10. Do we sometimes decide to get drunk and then go do it?
11. What prompts us?
12. Do we feel we have to admit it?
13. What do we come to understand when we drink deliberately?
14. At this stage of the disease, can we imagine the consequences when we start drinking?
15. To whom do the first 100 compare our behavior?
16. What really thrilled this guy?
17. Was he having fun?
18. Did his actions bother his friends?
19. How did people label him?
20. What happed when his luck ran out?
21. If he were a normie, what would he have done?
22. Since he wasn't normal, what happened?
23. What did he decide to do?
24. What were the consequences for his inability to quit for good?
25. Did he keep on trying to quit?
26. Did his problem cost him his job?
27. Did it cost him his wife?
28. Did it make a fool of him?
29. Did he try everything to quit?
30. How far did he go to quit jay-walking?
31. What happened the day he left lock up?
32. What label would you put on this guy?
33. Is this illustration ridiculous?
34. What will we real alcoholics admit?
35. As intelligent as we are, what do we honestly admit?
36. Is it true or false?
37. What do some alcoholics think?

1. Who can stay sober on self-knowledge?
2. How well can the actual or potential alcoholic stay away from drinking based on this self-knowledge?
3. What point do we want to drive home to the alcoholic?
4. What was Fred's profession?
5. Was he in good shape materially?
6. How was his home life?
7. What kind of personality did he have?
8. How was his business life?
9. Did he appear to be a normal person?
10. Was he doing well in his life?
11. What was his one problem?
12. When had the AA's first seen Fred?
13. Where did they meet him?
14. Why did he say he was there?
15. Had he experienced this before?
16. How did he feel about it?
17. Could he admit he was alcoholic?
18. How did he rationalize it?
19. What did the doctor try to impress on him?
20. How were his spirits?
21. What decision did he make?
22. Did he have any doubt that he could handle that decision?
23. Was he successful at every other area of his life?
24. What would Fred not do?
25. What couldn't Fred not accept?
26. What did the AA's tell him?
27. Did he express any interest?
28. To what did he concede?
29. He was a long way from what?
30. What was he certain he could do after the knowledge the AA's had given him?
31. What did Fred believe would fix him?
32. A year later, what were the AA's told?
33. In what condition was he in?
34. Who did he want to see?
35. What was his excuse for drinking?
36. What was he impressed with?

37. What did he not believe?
38. What ideas impressed him the most?
39. What was he confident in?
40. What was his reasoning?
41. Why did he feel self-confident that he could manage his decision to not drink again?
42. What did he do in that frame of mind?
43. How was everything going?
44. What did he have trouble with?
45. How was it going?
46. What was he having trouble with?
47. What did his alcoholic mind begin to wonder?
48. Where did he go on business?
49. Was this a new experience?
50. How was he physically?
51. What problems did he have?
52. How did his business in Washington go?
53. What kind of day had it been?
54. How was business in Washington?
55. What did he do at the end of business for the day?
56. In the dining room, what insane thought did he have?
57. How did he react to that insane thought?
58. What did he do then?
59. After dinner what happened?
60. After returning to the hotel, what did he do?
61. He remembered what after the third drink?
62. He then had a vague recollection of what?
63. Who did he meet up with at the landing field?
64. What did they do and for how long?
65. What did he remember of all this?
66. Where did he wind up and with what?
67. After his mind cleared, what did he do?
68. Had he resisted the first drink?
69. Was he conscious of the fact he had taken a drink?
70. How was he drinking?
71. What did he remember his AA friends had said?

1. What did they say would happen even with his determination not to drink?
2. How well did his self-knowledge work?
3. What did he come to know?
4. What did he learn about self-knowledge and willpower?
5. What else did he come to understand?
6. How did this newly acquired knowledge affect him?
7. Who came to see him?
8. What was the first thing they did?
9. What did Fred think of what they did?
10. What two questions did they ask Fred?
11. To what did he concede?
12. What did they pile on him?
13. What did this do for him?
14. Once he admitted defeat, what did they tell him?
15. Did he have difficulty accepting the program?
16. How did he feel about putting the program into action?
17. What would he have to do?
18. Was it going to be easy?
19. What happened to Fred as soon as he decided to adopt the program?
20. What else did he discover?
21. What kind of life did the new decision bring?
22. What was his old life like?
23. What would he not trade for?
24. Would he have liked to return to his old way of living?
25. What does Fred's story do?
26. What are our hopes?
27. Had he severely suffered from alcoholism?
28. Do most alcoholics get off so easy?
29. How do many doctors and psychiatrists feel about alcoholism?
30. What did one professional say?

31. Once more, what?
32. Can humans provide the alcoholic a defense from the next drink?
33. What is an alcoholic's only certain defense?

More Facts

The delusion that the alcoholic can be like other people in regard to alcohol is exploded.

2.   The need to accept one's alcoholism is the first step in the recovery process.

3.   Again the fact that loss of control over drinking is the central and irreversible feature of alcoholism.

4.   A further analysis of the mental states that precede the first drink as states of temporary insanity.

5.   These states of temporary insanity do not yield to self-will nor to self- knowledge.

6.   Only a spiritual answer, only divine help, can save the alcoholic from incarceration, a mental hospital, or death.

CHAPTER 6

WE AGNOSTICS

Much has been made of the religious language in the *Alcoholics Anonymous* "The Big Book." Some conservatives cite this language as evidence that the Twelve Step program is really a Christian program that cannot be fully effective without an active faith in Christ. Others see this same language simply as a product of its time that does not play an important role in Twelve Step spirituality. Still others are threatened by the religious language of the Big Book and disregard the book as a whole because they feel it is aggressively religious.

It is common knowledge that AA, and therefore the entire Twelve Step movement, had its birth within and evangelical Christian movement known as the Oxford Group. AA separated itself from the Oxford Group prior to the publication of the Big Book. The founders decided they didn't want organized religion to block anyone out, for any reason. The Big Book contains some religious language, but only mentions Jesus once, and then only in passing. This has left historians and AA members divided over some important questions. Just how Christian was early AA? Who is the God of the Big Book? Is this the Christian God, or can we really take this to mean a God of our own understanding?

In its chapter, "We Agnostics," the Big Book outlines its attitude toward spiritual and religious matters. In doing so, the Big Book also presents a method by which readers can investigate theological questions for themselves. By exploring this method, we should be able to answer some questions about the nature of the Big Book's ideas about God. There are a few problems with the Big Book's theological method, and these must be taken seriously

The Big Book encourages its readers to adopt an attitude toward spiritual matters similar to the Wright brothers' attitude toward flight. The point being that the reader ought not preclude opportunities for spiritual recovery without giving them a fair trial. In an appendix on spiritual experience, the Big Book quotes Herbert Spencer to the effect that one can only be excluded from spiritual growth if one fosters an attitude of "contempt prior to investigation."

A common saying in AA meetings is, "Contempt prior to investigation is ignorance."

For "We Agnostics," the spiritual life begins in ignorance. The alcoholic is expected to start without any preconceived ideas about God, but simply a willingness to believe. This willingness allows the alcoholic to experiment with the Twelve Steps. In taking Steps, the alcoholic begins to have spiritual experiences, and these become the basis for a growing faith in spiritual power. The Big Book insists that it is impossible to fully understand or define this power, and so each alcoholic is free to come to their own understanding of God, based on their own spiritual experiences in the Twelve Steps. The Big Book's theological method begins with willingness, proceeds to action, from action to experience, from experience to faith, and finally conception. One important assumption of this method is that personal experience is a valid way to gain knowledge of spiritual things.

Here's a good question for the agnostic. "Can you go to the beach and stand there watching the waves break and the water moving and by your own power, stop the waves?

Each person will have their own unique experience and will arrive at their own unique understanding of God. This inevitably results in an environment of pluralism, wherein there is little agreement about theological issues.

"WE AGNOSTICS" is a remarkable piece of writing. Bill W was an agnostic four years before the chapter was written and he demonstrates the depth of understanding on how a hopeless alcoholic can receive spirituality.

The chapter begins with some of the most important info this book contains. We learn the truth about the fatal disease, alcoholism. The chapter gives us a test, that if answered honestly, will tell us that we need what this program has to offer. The test also gives us the true answer to our problem, a God or Higher Power, as we Understand Him.

The chapter helps us open our mind so that we can get a key ingredient to move forward, willingness. Once we have willingness, we are told that we will have what is necessary to have a relationship with our Creator. We also learn that our Higher Power is already inside us and we don't have to go searching for Him.

1. What have we learned so far?
2. What do we want to make clear?
3. How do you know if your life is unmanageable?
4. How do you know if you are powerless over alcohol?
5. If you cannot quit and have little control over your drinking, what are you?
6. What is the only known solution?

7. Will this present problems to an atheist or agnostic?
8. Especially if they are what type of alcoholic?
9. What is your destiny if you can't manage a decision after your first drink?
10. What is the alternative?
11. Are these alternatives easy for real alcoholics?
12. When can we see the truth, is it really so difficult to hope that there just might be a Higher Power?
13. How many of the first 100 where atheists or agnostics?
14. What do some of us try to do with the truth?
15. What are we hoping for?
16. Ultimately, what must we do?
17. Is it possible that this could apply to you?
18. What does our experience show to the atheist or agnostic?
19. Will a code of morals or a good philosophy save the real alcoholic?
20. If we really apply ourselves, can we resist the first drink?
21. When we use all our might and put our very best to work, what is still needed?
22. When we sincerely apply self-will to our human resources, how successful can we be?
23. What is lack of power?
24. To live, what did we have to do?
25. What did it have to be?
26. If that is what we must have to survive, what is the question?
27. Where do we find the answer to that most important question?
28. What is its main object?
29. This Power will do what?
30. This book is written to be what?
31. We are going to talk about who?
32. Who will have difficulty with this topic?
33. What will give the newcomer hope?
34. Why will this topic disturb him?
35. Do we understand?
36. What of his have we shared?

37. The word "God" does what to others?
38. Why did we reject a particular conception?
39. Once we rejected all ideas, what did we believe?
40. What was it that bothered us?

Page 46

1. What gave us cause to believe this?
2. Why did we distrust some?
3. With all the evil, what two questions were posed?
4. Yet, in other moments, what did we wonder?
5. What have we shared with people who have an agnostic temperament?
6. What do we want to hurry and do?
7. What happens when we are able to set aside our prejudices and become willing?
8. This happens even though what?
9. What were we relieved to learn?
10. If we are able to pretend in a Higher Power, what is promised?
11. What two things will we possess as soon as we are able to admit there might be a Higher Power?
12. Provided we do what?
13. What have we found?
14. We have found the "Realm of the Spirit" to be what?
15. Who may benefit by it?
16. When we speak of God, what do we mean?
17. How about other spiritual ideas in this Book?
18. What should we not do?
19. What else do we need at the start?
20. What will happen later?
21. What do we call that?
    What do we use?
    What question do we need to ask ourselves? (2 sentences)
22. As soon as we can say "yes" to that question,

where are we?
23. What has been proven?
24. Why was this great news for us?
25. When recovered alcoholics presented spiritual approaches to our problem, what did we say? (3 sentences)
26. What was it comforting to learn?
27. What were we unable to do?
    (Page 48)

28. What was our handicap?
29. How do many of us react to the mention of spiritual things?
30. Is this sort of thinking OK?
31. Even though some of us resisted the idea, what happened?
32. Faced with what?
33. We became what?
34. What persuaded us?
35. It did what?
36. Did this happen easily?
37. What is one of our hopes?
38. What may the reader still ask?
39. What kind of reasons are there?
40. What are we going to do?
41. Who likes facts and results?
42. At this point in history, what are we willing to accept?
43. They must be based on what?
44. What theory does Bill use as an example?
45. Who doubts this power?
46. Why? (2 sentences)
47.
    (Page 48 - continued)

48. Everybody now believes what?
49. But what is lacking?
50. What has science demonstrated?
51. What is constantly being revealed?
52. What is a steel girder?
    (Page 49)

53. Do we doubt this theory? (3 sentences)
54. What happens when someone wants to talk about God?
55. What thinking are we trying to support when we read books and engage in arguments?
56. If we were right, what would be true?
57. How should we consider ourselves?
58. How do some of us consider ourselves?
59. Is that rather egotistical of us?
60. Those of us who have been there and done it, what do we beg of the reader?
61. Even against what?
62. What have we learned?
63. What do people of faith have?
64. Did we have a clue as to what it was about?
65. How did we spend some of our leisure hours?
66. What could we have observed?
67. What should we have done?
    (Page 50)
68. Instead, what did we do?
69. We sometimes do what?
70. When we accused others of being intolerant, what were we?
71. Why did we miss the beauty of life?
72. What have some of us never done?
73. What will the reader find in our stories?
74. Do we have to agree with their approach?
75. What has experience taught us?
76. Who must answer these questions?
77. Do we agree on anything?
78. What is the one thing all recovered alcoholics agree on?
79. What produced this phenomenal agreement?
80. What are we going to do now?
81. Whose record are we going to look at?
82. What do they declare?
83. What besides "believing in" and having a "certain attitude" is necessary?
84. There has been a revolutionary change in what?
85. No matter how bad it got, what happened?
86. When did these remarkable promises take place?

(Page 51)

87. Once confused and baffled, we come to understand the reasons for what?

88. Ignoring the problems caused by our drinking, what did they come to see clearly ?

89. What do they demonstrate?

90. What is it that many recovered alcoholics are able to say?

91. What do they present?

92. What type of progress has our society made during this century?

93. Does everyone know why?

94. Are we more intelligent than our ancestors?

95. Why has material progress been so slow in previous centuries?

96. What controlled the minds of men in the past?

97. How did some folks feel about Columbus' idea that the world is round?

98. Why were folks angry with Galileo?

99. With these facts in mind, we ask ourselves what?

100. What was it that American newsmen were afraid to report?

101. What produced that fear? (2 sentences)

102. Was there mathematical proof to refute the truth?

103. People believed what?

(Page 52)

104. But what did happen in a very few years?

105. What is true in most fields today?

106. What is one thing that will characterize our present generation?

107. We are completely ready to do what?

108. What question did we have to ask ourselves?

109. With what were we having trouble?

110. Looking at the quality of our lives, what seemed to be most important?

111. When we saw others solve these problems, we had to do what?

112. How good are our ideas?

113. What did work?

114. What made it possible for the Wright brothers to be successful?

115. What would have happened without it?

116. What were the agnostics and atheists doing?

117. What did the recovered alcoholics show everyone?

(Page 53)

118. What is logic?

119. How do we feel about it? (2 sentences)

120. What have we been given?

121. Is it an asset or a liability?

122. What would an agnostic not be satisfied with?

123. What do we have difficulty in telling?

124. As hopeless alcoholics, what proposition must we face?

125. What choice must we make? (2 sentences)

126. With what are we now confronted?

127. Could we ignore it?

128. What have some of us already done?

129. What had given us fresh courage?

130. How were we welcomed?

131. How did we feel about our sense of reason?

132. What could we not do?

(Page 53 - continued)

133. What were we relying on?

134. What do we need to do at this point?

135. What had happened without us being aware of it?

136. What did we have confidence in?

137. That was a sort of what?

138. To what had we been faithful?

139. When was faith not a part of our daily lives?

140. What was the next thing we found?

141. How did that affect us?
142. What had we worshipped?
143. What feeling did we sometimes feel when we observed some of God's handiwork?
144. What was the next thing we learned?
145. What proved to be more powerful than our power of reasoning?
146. On what were our lives constructed?
147. Did acting on our feelings really shape our existence?
148. After reviewing the truth, what could we not say?
149. On what have we and do we live by?
150. What would life be without faith? (2 sentences)
151. Do we believe in life?
152. Can we prove life in a purely scientific manner?
153. Can we say the details of our universe mean nothing?
154. So, is our reasoning the last word?
155. How dependable is reasoning, the way we use it?

(Page 55)

156. How reliable was the best reasoning regarding man's ability to fly?
157. What kind of flight did we see in the Fellowship of Alcoholics Anonymous?
158. What did they say made it possible?
159. Did we feel a little pity for the poor misguided souls?
160. What did our sense of reasoning tell us?
161. Why were we fooling ourselves?
162. How is that reality hidden sometimes?
163. What are the real facts which are older than the history of mankind?

164. What do we finally come to see?
165. Must we search for Him?
166. What is as much a fact as we are?
167. Where, in the human life, may He be found?
168. Where is the only place we may come to know God?
169. We can only do a bit of what?
170. If you can believe our stories, you will be able to do what?
171. What promise comes with this attitude? (2 sentences)
172. Is there a story of an atheist in this Book?
173. Why is it being mentioned at this point?
174. Could it be that he had a spiritual experience as the result of trying this Program? (Page 56)
175. What kind of a childhood did this man have?
176. How had he come to feel about religious matters?
177. Was his life one of happiness and peace of mind?
178. What things did he experience?
179. How did they affect him?
180. But that was not all. What else?
181. Where did he wind up?

182. Who came to visit him?

183. How did the visit affect him?

184. But later, what did he ask?
185. How did he feel when he began to think maybe he had been wrong?
186. What thought overwhelmed him?
187. What did he do?

188. What happened almost immediately?

189. How did it feel to him?

190. What happened to his sense of reason?

191.   Where did he find himself?

192.   Had he stepped into the "World of the Spirit?"

193.   Of what was he now conscious?

194.   Was he now on solid ground?

195.   Had any drastic changes in his life altered his faith?

196.   What happened to his drinking problem?

197.   Did his Higher Power solve his problem? (Page 57)

198.   To what extent did the thought of drinking return to him?

199.   How did he react to those brief moments?

200.   Had he now joined the First 100 as being a recovered alcoholic?

201.   Had the hope of Step Two become a reality in his life?

202.   What do we call this type of event?

203.   Are its elements complex?

204.   What made it possible for him to come to believe?

205.   What did he do?

206.   Then he what?

207.   For how many had God repeated this miracle?

208.   Did this man have a spiritual awakening or a spiritual experience?

209.   Then some of us must experience which?

210.   What is the promise to all those who will become students and practitioners of this Basic Textbook?

211.   If we try to apply these Steps to our lives, what will happen?

MAIN POINTS

1. The alcoholic needs to find a power greater than himself.
2. What power greater than self is wide open, but there must be an appeal to some power greater than the conscious self.
3. It is the practical effect of such a belief as shown in the stories in the Book of AA that commend such a belief.
4. The belief in a power greater than self and a set of actions described in subsequent chapters works.

CHAPTER 7

HOW IT WORKS (58-71)

In "How it Works," we have a deeper understanding of the disease of alcoholism. We are learning that the solution is found in God, as we understand him. In this chapter we perceive our first set of directions for Steps 3 and 4.

We start by reading that this Program works for those who apply it. We are also told why it fails for some. We are also given more spiritual principles and prayers.

Bill W started writing this chapter and realized he was missing some vital information. He had the 6 precepts that started with the "Oxford Group".

1. Complete deflation.
2. Dependence and guidance from a Higher Power.
3. Moral inventory.
4. Confession.
5. Restitution.
6. Continued work with other alcoholics.

Bill W believed that these were not enough, so he prayed. He set his pencil and pad down and gave 30 minutes to seek guidance through prayer and meditation. He then picked up his paper and pencil and started writing. His hand seemed to flow on its own. After writing for about 40 minutes, he checked out what he had written and placed numbers by the "Steps" and was pleasantly surprised to find that the 6 had become 12! Bill believed it was significant because of the 12 Apostles.

Bill W tells us that the Steps will help us break free from the insanity that leads the chronic alcoholic to drink? In fact, we believe that if we follow these suggestions, "Rarely have we seen a person fail who has thoroughly followed our path."

(P)   1. To be successful in this Program, what must we do?
       Who will not recover?
       What is usually their natural problem?

4. Are there such people?

5. Why are they that way?

6. What are they unable to do?

7. Are their chances pretty good?

8. What other types of alcoholics can recover?

(P)   9. What are our stories supposed to do?
        10. If you want what this program has to offer, what must you do?

(P)   11. Do we look forward to taking these Steps?

        12. With our sound sense of reasoning, what do we try to do?

        13. Could we find it?

14. What do we sincerely beg of you?

        Which of our old ideas, beliefs or opinions are worth retaining?
                15-b. What must we do with our old ideas?

(P)   17. What must we remember?
                (Page 59)
        1. Must we have help?
        2. Who has all the Power?
        3. When should we try to find Him?

(P)   4. If we are halfhearted in applying this program, how successful will we be?
        5. If we understand that lack of power is our Problem and that a Power greater than ourselves is the Solution, where are we?
        6. What do we ask?

(P)   7-a. Here are the Steps we what?
                7-b. What are these Steps?

Step 1. The Problem - alcoholism.

Step 2.   The Solution - a Power greater than ourselves.

Step 3.   A Decision to take the rest of the Steps to learn if that Power greater than ourselves is available to us.

(Page 59 - continued)

Step 4.   An effort to learn the Truth about ourselves.

Step 5.   The humility to honestly admit our character defects to our Higher Power, ourselves and another human being and to learn more of the Truth about the way we have treated and harmed others.

Step 6.   A commitment to our Higher Power that we will continue our study of the Big Book and follow the clear-cut directions to the best of our understanding.

Step 7. Now that we have told Him we will do our part, we humbly ask Him to do His part.

Step 8.   Take the list from Column One of our Fourth Step and add to it all the people we have neglected, used, abused or otherwise harmed.

Step 9.   Make restitution to all those on our Step Eight list of people we have harmed.

Step 10. Continue to apply Steps 4, 5, 6, 7, 8 and 9 moment by moment, day by day.

Step 11. This is how we learn to talk to God (pray) and listen to God.

(Page 60)

Step 12. This is the Promise of the Program, the statement of our Primary Purpose and how we are to apply these Steps to every area of our lives. This is where we live the Program.

1-a. What is the promise of having taken the first eleven Steps?
1-b. What must we then try to do?
1-c. Where else must we apply these Steps?

(P)   4. What do many of us exclaim?

5. Should we just throw our hands up and quit?

6. How many of us are doing this *precisely*?

7. We certainly are not what?

8. If we really want to recover, we must be willing to do what?

9-a. What is the nature of these Twelve Steps?
9-b. What are they designed to do?

11-a. What do we gain as the result of taking these Steps?
11-b. But we will never achieve what?

(P)   13-a. What two Sections of this Book describe the alcoholic?
13-b. What chapter describes the Agnostic?
13-c. Where do we find the adventures, before and after?

(Page 60 - continued)

13-d. What do these make clear?

(a) Is this Step One?
(b) Is this also Step One?
(c) Is this Step Two?

(P)   17-a. If we are convinced of these vital issues, the (a), (b), (c)'s, where are we?
                17-b. What have we decided to do?

        19. Which two questions need to be answered at this point?

(P)   20. What is the first requirement in answering the "first question?"

        21. Why is that?

        22.   Everybody is like what?

(Page 61)
        1-a. What do we want regarding our plans and people's actions?
        1-b. If everyone played his part, how would our life be?
        3. How would everybody feel and how would life be?
        4. In writing the script for all the players, is the actor sometime noble?
        5. He might even be what?
        6. But then he may be what?
        7. If he is like most people, how will he be?

(P)   8. What usually happens? (2 sentences)

        9. What does he begin to think?

        10. What does he decide to do?

        11. How does he change his approach?

12. Is he now pleased with the results?

13. Who gets the blame?

14. How does this make him feel?
15. What is his basic trouble? (2 sentences)

16. He is the victim of what illusion?

17. What should be evident to all the other people in his life?

18. How do his actions affect the other people in his life?

19. What is usually the product of his efforts?

(P)   20. What would people call our actor?

21. He can be compared to whom?
(Page 62)
1. With all our fussing and complaining, what are we really concerned with?

(P)   2. What is the root of our troubles? (2 sentences)

3-a. What manifestations of our selfishness drive us?
3-b. What do we do?
3-c. And they do what?

6. When people hurt us, seemingly without any provocation on our part, what do we usually find?

(P)   7. Who is really responsible for all our troubles?

8-a. Where do they come from?
8-b. What is the alcoholic an extreme example of?
8-c. Can the alcoholic see the truth?

11. Above everything, what has to happen?

12. Why is that so important?
13. How is that possible?

14. What alternatives are there?

15-a. Do many of us have a high standard of values?
15-b. How well do we live up to our own values?

17. What can we not reduce through our own willpower?

18.   We must have what?
                (Page 62 - continued)

(P)   19. What is the first thing we must do?

20. Why?

21. What did we then decide?

22. If He is the Principal, what are we?

23. If He is the Father, what are we?

24-a. What are most good ideas?
24-b. What does this decision prove to be?
24-c. Through which we pass to what?

(Page 63)
(P)   1. What happens when we become serious about this Program?

2. What did we now have?
        3-a. He is what?
        3-b. What will our new Boss promise to do?

3-c. What must we do?
    6. Established on this footing, what is promised?

        7. As we feel the new Power flow in, what else is promised?

        8. We are what?

(P)   9. Is it now time to make a decision to really try the Program by taking the Steps?

            10-a. I give myself to Whom?
                        10-b. For what purpose?

        12-a. What do I want relief from?
        12-b. Why would I want to be free of my selfishness?

            (Page 63 - continued)

        14-a. What else do I want to be free of?
        14-b. Why do I pray that they will be removed?

    16. How long do I really want to do His will?

    17. What must we do before taking this Step?

(P)   18. HOW do we take this Step?

            19-a. Must we pray this prayer exactly as written?
            19-b. If we reword it, can we leave out part of the meaning?

            21-a. If every action begins with a decision, are we now ready to begin?
            22-b. If honestly and humbly prayed,

WHAT will be the results?

(P)   23-a. Now that we have decided to take
the Steps, how do we go about it?
          23-b. What is the first step in carrying out
the decision?

(Page 64)
          1-a. What was our Third Step decision?
          1-b. What is necessary for the effect to be
a lasting one?
          1-c. When should we do Step Four?

          4. Was alcohol our problem?

          5. What did we have to determine?

(P)   6. What did we start?

          7. What happens to a business that takes no
inventory?

          8. What is a commercial inventory?

          9. What is the purpose of an inventory?

          10. What is the main object of an inventory?

          11. If the owner is to be successful, what is it he
must not do?

(P)   12. What do we do?

          13. How do we take stock of ourselves?

          14. What are we looking for?

          15-a. What had defeated us?
          15-b. What do we consider?

(P) 17 What is the first manifestation of our character defects we look at?

Question - What is a resentment?

Answer – Remembering a previous situation that made us angry and re-feeling the anger that it produced.

18. What does it do to alcoholics?

(Page 64 - continued)

20-a. From it comes what?

20-b. In how many ways are alcoholics ill or sick?

22. When we have a spiritual awakening or spiritual experience, what is promised?

23. Do we need a pad of paper and a pencil or pen?

24. What is the first thing we list on the pad of paper?

(Column one: *I'm resentful at:*)

25. What is the next thing we ask of ourselves?
(Column two: *The Cause)*

26. What did we find to be true in most cases?

(Page 65)

1. So, what were we?

(P)   2. What do we then set down opposite the ones we resent?

(Column three: *Affects my:*)

3. What do we list in Column three?

(P)   4. How definite should we be?

(P)   5. How far back do we go in listing those we resent?

6. Only what counts in doing our inventory?

7. When we are finished, what do we do?

8. What is the first thing that becomes apparent as we study what we have done?

(Page 66)
1. Is that where most of us stop?

2. What continues to happen?

3. What was it sometimes and then who were we mad at?

4. The harder we tried to have our way, what happened?

5. Did we win some battles and lose the war?

(P)   6. What becomes plain?

7. What is the result of thinking about what they did to us and how we are going to get even with them?
8-a. What is the hope of the alcoholic who is trying this program?
8-b. Are resentments a serious matter to alcoholics?
10. How serious are they?

11. What do we give up by replaying our resentments?

12. What happens then?

13. Does the alcoholic quit drinking then?

(P)   14. If we are going to live, what must happen?

15. Is thinking about the way we can get even OK for alcoholics?
>16-a. How about for non-alcoholics?
>16-b. But for alcoholics, they are what?

(P)   18-a. What do we go back to?
>18-b. What does it hold for us?
>20. What are we now prepared to do?

21. What do we begin to see?
(Page 66 - continued)

22. Does it make any difference whether or not the event that caused the resentment actually happened?

23. What did we see?

24. Can we carry out a decision to drop all our resentments and forget them?

(P)   25. What will be our course?

(Page 67)
1. What did we see about the ones who offended us?

2. What do we ask God?

3. When a person hurts us, what do we pray?
(P)   4. What do we avoid?

5. Why do we avoid that?

6. What might happen if we do?

7-a. Can we help everyone?
7-b. What is the promise of the "Resentment Prayer?"

(P)   9. What do we do next?

10-a. As we begin, what do we disregard?
10-b. Whose mistakes do we look at?

12. What, specifically, are we looking for?
13. Though the situation had not been entirely our fault, what do we try to do regarding the other person?

14. Is it all right to place some of the blame on them?

15. We are looking for what?

16. Whose inventory is this?

17. What do we do as soon as we see our faults?
(Page 67 - continued)

18. What is promised as the result of closely following the directions?

(P)   19. What part of our lives does fear touch?
20. Is it a part of our existence?

21. What does it set in motion?

22. Who is responsible for the fear we experience?

1. How can we classify fear?
2. Why?

(P)   3. What do we do with our fears?

     4. Do we write them down?

     5. What do we ask ourselves?

     6. Does self-reliance have anything to do with it?

     7. How good is self-reliance?
         8-a. What did some of us once have?
         8-b. What did it solve?
   10. What made it worse?

(P)   11. What do we think about this matter?

     12. What different basis are we now on, having started carrying out our Third Step decision?

     13. Who do we now trust?

     14. What is our role in life now?

     15-a. Just to the extent we do what?
     15-b. If we really let Him direct our life, what is promised?

(P)   17. When and to whom do we apologize for our new way of life?

     18. We can laugh at who?
         (Page 68 - continued)

     18. What does faith produce?

     19. What do all men of faith possess?

20. In Whom do they place their trust?

21. When do we apologize for our dependence upon our Higher Power?

22. What do we let Him do?

23. What do we ask of Him when we experience fear?

24. What are we promised will, at once, begin to happen?

(P)   25. What do many of us need when it comes to our sex conduct?

26. Above all, we try to do what?

27. Is it easy to mess up here?

28. What kind of opinions do we encounter when it comes to this topic?

29. One side of the debate looks at sex as what?

(Page 69)
1. What is the other side of the debate?

2. What do they think?

3. What do they see?
        4-a. One side would allow what?
        4-b. The other side would allow what?
6. Do we want to set these people straight?

7. Do we want to be the judge of anyone's sex conduct?

8. Who has sex problems?

9. What would we be if we didn't?

10. So now, what is the question?

(P)   11. We begin this part of our inventory by doing what?

12. What are we looking for?

13. Of whom do we make a list?

14. Do we add those to our list who have been hurt by some more subtle actions on our part?

15-a. Whose wrong do we examine?
15-b. What do we ask ourselves?

17. Do we put all this on paper just as we did the manifestations of our other personality defects?

(P)   18. By doing this, what are we really trying to do?

(Page 69 - continued)

19. What test do we apply?

20. What do we ask of God?

21-a. What must we remember about the source of our sex   powers?
21-b. They are therefore what?
21-c. They are not to be used how?

(P)   24-a. Are we to determine our ideals regarding our sex conduct?
24-b. Again, what is the key to success in this area of our lives?

26-a. We must also be willing to do what?
26-b. Provided that in doing so, we do not

do what?

28. How do we treat sex in our program?

29. What do we ask of God?

30. What is the promise of that prayer?

(P)   31. Who can judge our sex situation?

32-a. What may be desirable?

(Page 70)
1-b. Who will be our final judge?
2. What have we come to realize?

3. What do we avoid?
(P)   4. If we fail, are we doomed to start drinking?

5. What do some folks think?

6. But is that true?

7. On what does it depend?

8. If we have a slip in our sex conduct, what attitude had we better have?

9. If we are not remorseful, and we continue to do what we want rather than what we know we should, what will happen?

10. Is this someone's theory?

11. How can we be so sure?

(P)   12. We earnestly pray for what?

        13. If sex continues to be a problem, what are we
told to do?

                (Page 70 - continued)

        14. What do we try to think of?

        15. What does this do?

                16-a. It will quiet what?
                16-b. If we yield, what will it mean?

(P)   18. If we have been thorough, what have we
done?

        19. What have we listed?

        20. What have we begun to understand?

        21. We have commenced to see what?

        22. We are promised that we will begin to learn
what?

                23-a. We have a list of who?
                23-b. And we are promised that we will be
willing to do what?

(P)   25. What do we read in this Book, over and over?

                (Page 71)

1.: Is this a self-help program or a God-help Program?

        2. Of what should we now become convinced?

3. If you have taken the Third Step and the Fourth Step, where are you?

5. What, then, have you learned?

MAIN POINTS

1. The specific studies outlined in the Twelve Steps are introduced.
2. The only program of spiritual development that has to do with stopping alcohol and other addictions.
3. How to work the first four Steps

CHAPTER 8

INTO ACTION (72-88)

We have now taken Steps 3 and $ and have given the willingness to put the AA Program to the test. Why not? We sure challenged ourselves in our addictions to go to great lengths to stay stuck in the bottle, so now we are going into action in the other direction. The title of Chapter 6 is "Into Action". In this chapter we are given more directions, more prayers and the Promises for Steps 6, 7, 8, 9, 10 and 11.

The simplicity of the Program is a key to maintain for happy recovery. We are told how to make our decision on page 63. From page 64 through page 83 we are told what we must do to be assured of a spiritual awakening and experience. We are also told that once we have taken these actions, we are now RECOVERED alcoholics. We get some more precious information in pages 84-88 where we learn how to take a daily inventory by applying Step 10 and finding the Power of God's (Higher Power's) will for us in Step 11.

(Pages 72 through 88)

Now that we have taken Steps Three and Four and have decided to put the Program of Alcoholics Anonymous to the test, we are ready to go into action.

That just happens to be the title of Chapter 6, "INTO ACTION". In this Chapter, we are given the directions, the prayers and the Promises for Steps Five, Six, Seven, Eight, Nine, Ten and Eleven.

What seems to be so amazing about this Program is its simplicity. We are told how to make our decision to begin recovery on page 63. From page 64 through page 83, we are told what we must do to be assured of a spiritual awakening or a spiritual experience. Once we have taken the action outlined in these pages, we are told we are now **recovered** alcoholics.

To maintain that miracle and to grow spiritually, we are told how we can take care of the moment by applying Step Ten and how to gain the Power and Knowledge of His will for us by practicing Step Eleven. That precious information is contained in just 5 pages (Pages 84 through 88).

Having followed the clear-cut directions presented in these 24 pages of this Basic Text, we are promised that we will have a spiritual awakening and thereby have a Solution for all our problems. Not just the problem of alcoholism, but ALL our problems.

The only way to see if that will prove true for us, as it did the authors of this Book, is to do what they report they did. With Step Four, we have taken only the first action Step. Now it is time for action and more action.

We recover by the Steps we take.

(Page 72)

(P)   1. Having completed our Fourth Step, what is the question?

2-a. What have we been trying to do?
2-b. And what else?
2-c. And discover what?

5-a. What have we admitted?
5-b. What have we ascertained?
5-c. We have put our finger on what?

8. What is about to happen to these defects of character?
9-a. What is required?
9-b. When completed, we will have admitted to whom?
9-c. And what will we have admitted?

12. Where are we at this point?

(P)   13. What is difficult about Step Five?

14. Do some of us feel that Step Four was enough truth?

15. What do we find in actual practice? (2 sentences)

16. Do many of us believe that we must do more?

17. Will some good reasons help us to be more willing to take this Step?

18. What is the very best reason for doing so?

19. Do many try to keep a secret or two?

20. Do they try to find an easier, softer way?

21. What almost invariably happens to them?

(Page 73)

1. Since they took Step Four, what did they wonder when they found themselves drunk?

2. What do we think the reason is?

3. Even though they made an attempt at Step Four, what had they done?

4. What *thoughts* did they hang onto?
5-a. What had they not learned?
5-b. What do they need to do?

(P)　　7. How many lives do alcoholics live?

8. What are we good at?

9. Do we put on a good front for the people in our lives?
(2 sentences)

10-a. If we are good at it, what do we enjoy?

10-b. Do we deserve it?

(P)　　12. What makes things worse?

13. When he comes out of a blackout, what happens?

14. What are these memories to him?

15. What really scares him?

16. What does he do with these memories?

17. What is his hope?

18-a. What does this do to him constantly?
18-b. This leads to what?
Page 73 - continued)

(P)   20. Do psychologists believe we are liars?

21. Do we pay them well to tell them half- truths and ignore their advice? (3 sentences)

22. Who were we willing to be honest with?

23. Is this one of the reasons members of the medical profession have such a low opinion of us?

(P)   24-a. What must we do?

(Page 74)

1-b. Why must we be entirely honest with someone?
2. Should we be careful about who we take Step Five with?

3. If our religious convictions require a confession, should we adhere to that?
4. If we have no religious connections, is it all right to go to a member of the clergy?
5. Do we sometimes find those who come to understand what we are trying to do?
6. On the other hand, do we sometimes find folks who want to change our Program?

(P)   7. If we don't want to go to a member of the clergy, what can we do?

8. What professionals might be acceptable?

9-a. What about a family member?
9-b. What can we not do if we use a family member or close friend?

11. What is it that we have no right to do?

12. How do we handle some parts of our story?

13. What rule do we follow?

(P)   14. What situation could exist?
15-a. What do we do if there is no one we can share with?
15-b. But we must be ready to do what?

17. Why do we say this?

18-a. What is important about the person who will hear our Fifth Step?
18-b. What must the person hearing our Fifth Step understand?
18-c. And they must not do what?
(Page 75)
1. Can we use this as an excuse to postpone?

(P)   2. WHEN do we do our Fifth Step?

3-a. What do we have?
3-b. We are prepared for what?

5. What do we explain to the person who is to hear us?

6. What must that person realize?

7. How will most people feel about doing this for us?

(P)   8. HOW do we take our Fifth Step?

9. If we are completely honest and thorough, WHAT is the first promise?

10. WHAT is the second promise?

11. WHAT is the third promise?

12. WHAT is the fourth promise?

13. WHAT is the fifth promise?

14. WHAT is the sixth promise?

15. WHAT is the seventh promise?

16. WHAT is the eighth promise?

(P)   17-a. Returning home, what do we do and for how long?

17-b. We very carefully do what?

(Page 75 - continued)

19. Why do we thank God?

20-a. What do we do then?
20-b. We turn to what page?

22-a. What do we do then?
22-b. What do we ask for?
22-c. What are we in the process of building?

25. Is it really important that we do this

thoroughly? (4 sentences)

(Page 76)

(P)   1. If we know we have done the very best we can, have held back no secrets in Steps Four & Five, we can look at what? (The WHEN)

      2. What have the First Hundred emphasized as absolutely necessary? (The HOW)

      3. Are we really ready to have God do what?

      4. What question is running through our mind at this point?
           (The WHAT)

      5. If we have one or more character defects we are unwilling to part with, what do we do?

(P)   6. WHEN we are ready, what do we do? (The HOW)

      7. What parts of our lives are we willing to let Him take?

      8. What do we ask Him to remove?

      9. We ask Him to grant us what?

      10. How do we know we have completed this prayer?

      11. What more do we do with Step Seven?

(P)   12-a. What do we now need? (The WHEN)

      12-b. Why do we need it?

      14. What Steps will we look at now?

15. What do we have?

16. Where did it come from?

17. What do we now do?

18. Why do we go to see our family, friends, and neighbors?
       (The HOW)

19. What do we really try to do? (The WHAT)

20. What do we pray for?

21. What must we remember? (The WHY)

(P)   22. What is probably true?

       23-a. As we review the list, how do we feel about some of them?
       23-b. Why might we feel that way?

25. Can we be assured?

26. Should we try to impress everyone of our spiritual way of life?
       (Page 77)
       1. If we get heavy on spirituality, how might that affect them?

2. What are we really trying to do?

3. Is that just what this program is all about?

4. What is the real purpose of the Twelve Steps of Alcoholics Anonymous?
5. What wouldn't be a very smart thing to do?

6. To do so would be like doing what?

7.   If we do, what may they think of us?

8. What is a far more important reason?

9. What will the person be impressed by?

10. What will the person be interested in?
(P)   11. We don't use this as an excuse for shying away from what?

12. If it can help, what are we willing to do?

13. What question will arise?

14. What if he has hurt me more than I have hurt him?

15. Nevertheless, what do we do?

16. Even though it is difficult going to an enemy, what are the
        results?
                (Page 77 - continued)

        17-a. In what frame of mind do we go to him? (The WHEN)
                17-b. What do we confess? (The HOW)

(P)   19. When can we criticize someone?

20. Very simply, what do we tell them?

        21-a. Why are we trying to make restitution?

                (Page 78)
        1-b. Do we then tell them what they should do?
        2. Whose faults are to be discussed? (2 sentences)
        3. If we do this in an unemotional and honest

manner, what will
    happen?

(P)   4. What happens most of the time?

    5. What happens sometimes?

    6. What rarely fails to happen?

    7. Sometimes, what do our enemies do?

    8. Occasionally, they will do what?

    9. But, does it really make any difference what
their reactions are?

    10. What counts? (2 sentences)

(P)   11. Most of us owe what?

    12. Do we shy away from those we owe?
        13-a. Are we honest with them?
        13-b. What do they usually know?

    15. Are we afraid to talk about our alcoholism?

    16. If we are open and honest with them, what
often happens?

    17. How do we go about settling our financial
amends?

    18. What caused the need for these amends?

        19-a. What must we lose?
        19-b. Why is this so important?
            (Page 78 - continued)

(P)   21. Have some of us committed criminal
offenses?

22. Have some of us "borrowed" money from our employers?

23-a. Have we told our sponsors about these things?
23-b. Yet, we are fearful of what?

25. Have some of us cheated on our expense accounts?

26. Do only a few of us do that sort of thing?

(Page 79)
1. Have some of us skipped payments on alimony or child support?
2. If so, may this have put us in trouble with the law? (2 sentences)

(P)   3. Although these amends take on many forms, what will we be given?
4-a. What must we remember?
4-b. What do we pray for?
4-c. May our efforts to make restitution produce some inconveniences?

7-a. What might be the consequences?
7-b. But we must be what?

9. Is this optional? (2 sentences)

(P)   10. If other people might be involved, what are we not to do?
(2 sentences)

11. Why was he behind in alimony? (2 sentences)

12. How did she feel about it and what did she do? (2 sentences)

13-a. Was he applying the Twelve Steps of

Alcoholics Anonymous to his life?
13-b. Was his life improving?

15. What could he have done?

(P)   16-a. How did we feel about him going to
jail?
        16-b. What would be the problem with
that, so far as making restitution?

18.   His sponsor suggested that he do what?

        19-a. Did he do what his sponsor told him
to do?
        19-b. What else did he do?
        (Page 79 - continued)

21. What did he promise?

22. What did he tell her he was willing to do?

23. What was the outcome?

(Page 80)

(P)   1. If other people might be affected, what do we
do?

        2-a. If they give permission, what is the
first thing we do?
        2-b. After talking with our sponsor, what
is the next step?
        2-c. If it needs to be done, what do we
not do?

(P)   5. What was the wrong that had to be righted?

(P)   6. Did he believe there was any way he could
make amends?

7. If he made it known, for whom did he fear?

8. What was the question facing him?

(P)   9-a. Who did he talk to about this problem?

9-b. After talking with them, what conclusion did he arrive at?

11-a. What did he see he had to do?
11-b. What did he know would happen if he didn't make the amend?

13. How did he make this amend?

14. What were the results?

(P)   15.   What is the next type of problem to be examined?

16. What would we, perhaps, not like to have generally known?

(Page 81)
1. Are alcoholics the only ones that do this sort of thing?

2. What does drinking do to our sex life at home?

3. Living with a drinking alcoholic does what to a wife?

4. Can she help it?

5. As she withdraws, what goes on with him?

6. He starts doing what?

7. What may he have going, hopefully unknown to interested parties?

8. What does a man doing this sort of thing normally feel?

(P) 9. Whatever the situation, we normally do what?

10. If the wife doesn't know, what do we generally do?

11. If she does know in a general way, what should we do?
      (2 sentences)
12. If she wants to know all the details, what do we do?

13. How do we feel about what we have done?

14. What else can we do?
      15-a. May there be exceptions?
      15-b. Do we consider the foregoing a rule?
      15-c. Is the preceding suggestion based on opinions or on experience?

(P) 18. Is our Program just for the alcoholic?

19. Who else can profit by it?

20. If we can forget, what about her?
      (Page 82)
   1. What is the best thing to do?

(P) 2. Some cases may demand what?
   3. Who, besides the couple, can decide?
   4. What may happen?

   5. What might each do?

6. We must remember we are dealing with what emotion?

7. Good generalship may do what?

(P)   8. If infidelity is not an issue, are we home free?

9. What really stupid thing do we all too often hear from an alcoholic?

10. Where is he with regard to his amends to his family?

11. What passes all understanding?

12. Had it not been for our families, where would many of us be?

(P)   13. The alcoholic is like what?

14. What are some of the results?

15. What has caused disharmony in the home?

16. An alcoholic is really unthinking when he says what?

17. What analogy do the First Hundred give us to help us see the havoc we have caused?

18. What did the farmer say to his wife that got him in big trouble?

(Page 83)

(P)   1. What lies ahead?

2. Who must lead the way?

3. Is an apology sufficient?
4-a. What should we do?
4-b. What should we not do?
6. If they are messed up emotionally, who may be partly to blame?

7-a. So what do we do?
7-b. WHEN do we ask?
7-c. For WHAT do we ask?

(P)   10. What is not a theory?

11. What must we do?

12. What if the family doesn't care for our program?

13. What should we not do?

14. Is there hope for them?

15. What will make an impression on them?
16. What must we remember?

(P)   17. Can we right all wrongs?

18. We don't worry about the wrongs we can't make right if what?

19. How do we make amends to those we cannot see?

(Page 83 - continued)

20. Can we postpone in some cases?

21. If a delay can be avoided, do we wait?

22. In making our amends, we should be what?

23-a. As God's kids, we do what?
23-b. What do we not do?

26. WHAT is the second promise?

27. WHAT is the third promise?

28. WHAT is the fourth promise?

(Page 84)

1. WHAT is the fifth promise?

2. WHAT is the sixth promise?

3. WHAT is the seventh promise?

4. WHAT is the eighth promise?

5. WHAT is the ninth promise?

6. WHAT is the tenth promise?

7. WHAT is the eleventh promise?

8. WHAT is the twelfth promise?

(P)   9. Are these promises overstated?

10. WHAT is the thirteenth promise?

11-a. If they come quickly, what do we call them?

11-b. If they come slowly, what do we call them?

13. WHAT is the fourteenth promise?

(Page 84 - continued)
(P)   14-a. With this thought, where are we?
14-b. Which says we continue to do what?

16. Is this something we do in a lackadaisical

manner?

17. What New World have we now become a part of?

18. What is the next thing we do?

19. Will this happen suddenly?

20. How long must we continue to apply these Steps to our lives?

21. WHAT do we watch for?

22. When these are detected, WHAT do we do and WHEN?

23-a. WHAT is the next thing we do and WHEN?

23-b. And then we do WHAT and WHEN do we do it?

25. Then we resolutely do WHAT?

(Page 84 - further continued)

26. As we learn to apply Step Ten, WHAT is the first promise?

(P)   27. What is the second promise? And we have ceased doing WHAT?

28. The third promise? WHAT are we promised at this point?

29. What is the fourth promise? WHAT will we no longer care about?

30. What is the fifth promise? If tempted, HOW do we react?

(Page 85)

1. What is the sixth promise? HOW do we react around alcohol?

2. What is the seventh promise? HOW did we get such freedom?

3. What is the eighth promise? Do we send off for it?

4. The ninth promise? Are we either fighting temptation or hiding from where alcohol is served?
5. The tenth promise? HOW do we feel?

6. The eleventh promise? Have we taken the pledge?

7. The twelfth promise? Instead, WHAT has happened?

8. The thirteenth promise? WHAT happened to it?

9. The fourteenth promise? We are neither WHAT?

10. Are these promises based on someone's ideas or opinions?

11. The fifteenth promise? WHAT is required to keep these promises alive and well?

(P) 12. What is so easy for an alcoholic to do?
13-a. What lies ahead?
13-b. Why?

15. We are not what of alcoholism?

(Page 85 - continued)
16-a. What do we have?
16-b. What is it contingent on?
18. What must we carry every day?

19-a. Who do we want to serve?
19-b. Whose will?

21. Are these thoughts optional?
22. What can we now do?

23. Why are we now able to do that?

(P)   24-a. What do we receive?
             24-b. Where does this come from?

26. What are we promised if we carefully follow the directions is this Book?

27. What have we begun to be?

28. What have we started to develop?

29-a. Now that we have recovered, can we stop?

29-b. What must we do now?

(P)   31. What is Step Eleven?
       32.   Why shouldn't we be shy about prayer?

(Page 86)
1. What is required to make prayer work?
2. What would be easy?
3. How did the First Hundred believe they could help us here?

(P)   4. What do we do at bedtime?
       5. What is the first question we must answer? (What four things do we continue to look for? Step Four?)
             6. What is the second question we must answer?
                   (Steps Eight & Nine?)
             7. What is the third question we must answer? (Step Five?)

8. What is the fourth question we must answer?

(Love & Service to God and the people about us?)

9. What is the fifth question we must answer?

10. What is the sixth question we must answer?

11-a. What is the seventh question we must answer?
11-b. What is the eighth question we must answer?

13-a. What must we be careful not to do?
13-b. Why?

15. After meditating on these questions, what do we pray?

(Page 86 - continued)

(P)   16. What is the first thing we should do when we wake up in the morning?

17. What do we consider?

18. What prayer do we apply before we begin?

19-a. What can we do under these conditions?
19-b. Why did God give us brains in the first place?

21. Where will we now find our thought-life?

(P)   22. Considering the day ahead, what may we face?

23. What may we not be able to do?

24. What do we pray?

25. How do we begin to learn to practice quiet meditation?

   (2 sentences)

26. What will surprise us after we practice, practice, practice these directions?

   (Page 87)

1. What do hunches and inspirations become for us?

2. Why will we not be inspired all the time?

3. If we presume the contrary, what will happen?

4. What do we find?

5. Does it become important to us?

(P)   6-a. How do we conclude our period of quiet meditation?

6-b. What do we pray for?

8-a. We especially pray for what?
8-b. What are we careful not to pray for?

10. What may we conditionally pray for?

11. How do some of us waste our time?

12. Why?

(P)   13. If we have family or friends close by, what might we do?

14. If our religion places requirements on us, what do we do?

15. If we have no religious affiliation, what can we do?

16. What may we refer to?

17.   Where might we find some good suggestions for other reading material?

18. What should we be quick to do?

19. Should we take advantage of their generosity?

(P)   20. When we are upset or confused, what do we pray?

21-a. What must we remember all the time?

(Page 88)

1-b. What else do we humbly pray?

2. By doing so, what are we promised?

3. Will we be able to get more done?

4. Why will that be so?

(P)   5. What is the next promise?

(P)   6. We alcoholics are what?

7. How do we let God discipline us?

(P)   8. Is learning to take the first Eleven Steps the end of our actions?

9. What is there more of?

10. What is dead?

11. What is Chapter Seven about?

MAIN POINTS

1. This chapter emphasizes action in discussing Steps 5-11. It makes the distinction between thinking and doing and actually living the Program.
2. The Promises are outlined for doing the Steps and staying sober.
3. This is a daily practice.
4. A closer to God feeling is described.
5. Prayer and Meditation is incorporated into the Program.

CHAPTER 9

WORKING WITH OTHERS (89-103)

Now we have ended the debate on God, as we understand Him by going through Steps 1,2 and 3. We also got more clarity by working through Steps 4, 5, 6 and 7. By working through Steps 8, 9 and 10 we are able to flush out resentments, fear, greed and other dishonest character defects. We learned how to improve our conscious contact with God in Step 11.

At this point we have experienced a deeper spiritual experience and are ready to continue to move forward in recovery. The psychic change and personality shift is underway to recover from alcoholism and the underlying issues related to the disease.

In our gratitude for what God has done for us, we move into action to help others recover from addiction. This gives us a purpose and helps us in sobriety. In Chapter 7 we see clear directions on where to find those still suffering, how to qualify them and how to help them understand alcoholism.

We then move forward with instructions on how to become a "sponsor". In this experience, we further secure our own sobriety by passing on our experience, strength and hope. It is awesome to see a sponsor with a sponsor with a sponsor to really see this Program at work and the miracles therein.

(Pages 89 through 103)

(Page 89)
(P)   1. What does practical experience show us?

2. If all else fails, do what?
      3-a. Carry what?
      3-b. To whom?

5. Who else is able to help the suffering alcoholic?

6. Why are you able to do this?

7. Why is it so important from their viewpoint?

(P)   8. What will happen to your life?

9. What happens as the result of us doing what we must do to assure our sobriety?

10. Are you willing to take a risk on missing what this is really all   about?

11. What is the bright spot of our lives?

(P)   12. It is hard to believe, but it may be that some of us are not what?

13. Where do the First 100 suggest you start?
14. Why would you think they might be glad to help you with your?

15. Better not do what?

16. What two reasons are given? (2 sentences)
      17-a. Who can we learn something from?
      17-b. What can you do that they can't?
19. So we do what?

20. What is our real purpose?
(Page 90)

(P)   1. When you learn of a prospect, do what first?

2. When do we not bother to talk to him?

3. Why?

4. Who else should know this?

5. What position should the family take?

(P)   6. If they indicate they have a desire to stop drinking, what is a good first thing to do?

7. Why would we want to do this?

8. How can this help you?

(P)   9. Sometimes it is a good idea to do what?

10. Who is going to resist this idea?

11-a. Don't do what?
11-b. Unless what?

13. When is a good time to ask a prospect a very important question?

14. What question should the serious drinker be asked?

15. If the prospect says "yes" to the question, what should the family do then?

16-a. How should you be described to the prospect?
16-b. What condition should be met by the prospect?

(Page 90 - continued)

(P)   18. Should we go talk to the prospect whether or not they want to see us?

19. How should the family react if the drinker says, "no?"

20. What should they wait for?

21. What could we do in the meantime, if it seems appropriate?
(2 sentences)

22. What must the family decide?

(Page 91)
1-a. Encourage the family to what?
1-b. Why?

(P)   3. What else should the family not try to do?

4. When possible, how should we not meet the drinker?

5. What is a better introduction?

6. Do we oppose medical treatment for the drinker?

7. Who can best introduce the prospect to your possible solution?

(P)   8. When might you see him?

9. Who do we not want present at our first meeting?

10. Why is this a good idea?

11. It will let him what?

12. When do you really want to have your first talk with a serious drinker?

13. Why?

(P)   14. How do we want to first meet the prospect?

15. How do we begin?

16. Then start talking about what?

17-a. What do we tell him?
17-b. What are we hoping for?

19. If he starts talking, what do we do?
(Page 91- continued)

20. What will you learn initially?

21. What do we do if he doesn't want to talk?

22. Is this a good time to talk about our program of recovery?

23-a. If he seems to be serious about our conversation, what do we dwell on?
23-b. What are we careful not to do?

25. If he is enjoying the conversation, do what?

26. Encourage him to do what?

(P)   27. Once he sees that you know what you are talking about, what do we do?

(Page 92)
1. Tell him what?

2. Give him an account of what?

3. Show him that the mental twist does what?

4. What Chapter in this Book do we go to explain the insanity of alcoholism?

5. What will this do for him?

6. Will he maybe enter into a "can you top this?" dialogue?

(P)   7-a. What very important determination are we to make at this point?

7-b. If we suspect we have a real one, what do we begin to do?

9-a. What is the source of your information?

9-b. What do we try to show him?

11-a. What do we not do at this point?

11-b. Unless what?

13. What do we not call him, even though it is necessary that we have determined this?

14. What is important?

15. What do we do if he doesn't think he has a serious drinking problem?

16. Do we tell him the truth anyway?

18. Do we emphasize the powerlessness because of the allergy and the unmanageability because of the alcoholic mind?

(Page 92 - continued)

19. On what do we keep his attention focused?

20. What do we explain to him?

21. Are doctors anxious to tell their alcoholic patients the truth?

22-a. What can we do that the doctors are

reluctant to do?

22-b. Why is this so?

24. If we stick with the directions given here, what will very likely happen?

25. What will help you get his serious attention?

26. If we have done a good job of describing the disease to our protégé, what will he be curious to know?

(Page 93)

1. What do we let him do?

2. Tell him what?

3. Stress what?

4. What do we do if he is a non-believer?

5. He can choose what?

6. The main thing is that he be willing to do two things. What are they?

(P) 7. How should we talk about our Program?

8. What may happen if we start getting righteous?

9. Do we talk our Program or our convictions?

(P) 10. What if the prospect belongs to a religious organization and is well schooled in religion?

11. What will they be curious to learn?

12. What may they be proof of?
13. Faith must be accompanied by what?

14. What are we not going to talk about?

15. Congratulate him on what he does know, but to what do we draw his attention?
16. How could trying to carry this message by telling our story help them see the point we just tried to make?
17. We represent no what?
(Page 94)
1-a. We deal only with what?
1-b. They are what?

(P) 3. Do we then outline the Twelve Steps of Alcoholics Anonymous?

4. What is very important for them to realize?

5. In reality, who is certain to benefit?
6-a. What do we make plain?
6-b. Our hope for them is what?
8. We suggest what as being important?

9. What do we make clear?

10-a. It shouldn't bother us if they what?
10-b. Why is that so?

12-a. How should our talk with them be?
12-b. If it was, what might have happened?

14. What may we have disturbed them about?

15. Is that good or bad?

16. Why would that be so?

17. Why is it good to make them feel hopeless?

(P) 18. If the candidate rejects the program, should

we argue with them?
19. What should we not do?

20. What do we tell them?

21. Do we mention Alcoholics Anonymous?

22. If they show interest, what do we make sure they have before we leave?
(Page 95)

(P)   1. At this point, we leave unless what?

2. What do we give him?

3. If we do stay longer, who directs the conversation?
4. What if the new person wants to get going right now?

5. Why could it prove to be a problem?

6. To be most successful, we should display what kind of an attitude?
7-a. What is another thing we should never do?
7-b. We simply do what?
9. What do we show them?

10. We offer what?

11. What do we tell them at this point?

(P)   12. If they are not interested in our Program of recovery, what should we do?
13. What may happen, if we do and why?

(P)   14. If they appear to be sincere, what do we ask them to do?

15. After doing this, what must they do?

16. By all means, what should not be done?

17. To be successful in our Program, what must happen within the prospect?

(P)   18. What do we do if they think there is a better way?

19. Do we have the only path of recovery?

20. What should we point out to the alcoholic?

21. What do we do then?
(Page 96)
(P)   1. Should we be discouraged if they don't buy our Program?

2. What should we do?

3. If you do, what will happen?

4. How do some of us waste our time?

5. If we leave the "slipper" alone, what may happen?

6. Why should we not spend too much time on one who will not follow directions?

7.Was one of our Fellowship lucky at 12th Stepping efforts early on?
8. What did he say would have happened if he had kept wasting his time?

(P)   9-a. We are now going to make our second visit to our prospect. What have they done?
9-b. What are they ready to do?

11. Why can you give your protégé advice?

(Page 96 - continued)
12-a. Let them know that you are available to help them if they are ready to take which three Steps?

12-b. What if they want to work with someone else?

(P)   14. What if your prospect is broke and homeless? (2 sentences)

15. But we should not do what?

16. We might be willing to do what?

17. But be sure to do what?

18. Be certain of what two very important considerations?

19. How can we hurt his chances?

20. We can make it possible for what?

(Page 97)

1. If we provide too much physical and/or material help to the newcomer, it may do what?

(P)   2. If we do provide material support, be sure of what?

3. Why are we so anxious to help others?

4. Will an occasional effort do it?

5. How often should we be willing to help others?

6. What inconveniences might this impose on us?

(rest of paragraph)

(P)   7. What do we seldom do for the alcoholic?

8. What two reasons are stated for this?

(P)   9. What should we do for the family of the alcoholic who doesn't make it?

10. How should we react to them?

11. What should the family be offered?

12. If they choose to adopt our Program as a way of life, what extra benefit might they realize?

13. Even if the alcoholic isn't successful in sobriety, what will happen for the family?

(P)   14. For the alcoholic who is able and willing to try our way of life, what is normally needed or wanted?
(Page 98)
1. Where are the ones who put emphasis on material help?
2-a. Yet, what do we do?
2-b. What is the condition for doing so?
4. Is this inconsistent?

(P)   5. What is the question to be answered before we give?

6. Why is this so important?

7. If our service is only of a material nature, what is the result?

8. This leads them to what? (2 sentences)

9. What hard lesson have some of us had to learn to be successful in sobriety?

(P)   10. What idea do we try to burn into the consciousness of every newcomer?

11. What is the single condition for success?

(P)   12. What domestic problems may the newcomer have?

13-a. What is the first thing the alcoholic should do?
13-b. He should then explain what?
13-c. Then what should he do?

16. The above applies if he has a what?

17-a. Is the family normally free of faults?
17-b. If faults do exist within the family, how should this affect the newcomer?

19. What should he concentrate on?

20. What must be avoided?

21. Will this be easy to do for everyone?
(Page 99)

1. If the family is able to forego arguments and fault-finding for a few months in the early days of recovery, what will happen?

2. How about the really incompatible folks?

3. Little by little, what will happen?

4. What positive thing can happen then?

(P)   5. What often happens after the family sees the effect of our Program on the alcoholic?

          6-a. When will this happen?

          6-b. Provided the alcoholic does what?

      8. Are all of us perfect at this?

      9. What must we try to do?

(P)   10. What about divorce or separation?

      11. What must come first?

      12. What should the wife understand?

      13. If their relationship is to be successful, what must happen?

      14. This will mean what?

      15. Sometimes it is best to do what?

      16. What rules apply here?

      17. What must the alcoholic do?

      18. What will become apparent to both parties if they apply this Program to their lives?

(P)   19. Let no alcoholic get by with saying what?

      20. Why?

      21. What may be true in some cases?

      22.   The newcomer must remember what?

(Page 100)

1. What is our success dependent upon?
2. What does our experience prove?
3. What else has others' experience proven?

(P)   4. What must you and your protégé do?

5. If you both stick with it, what will happen?

6. What has our experience shown us?
     7-a. If we follow the dictates of our
Higher Power, what will happen?
          7-b. That will be true regardless of what?

(P)   9. When we are working with a new man and
his family we must do what?
     10. Why?

11. Try to help the man's family do what?

12. What should they be warned against?

13. What should we help the family understand?

14. Help them see what?

15. What should they, hopefully, remember?

(P)   16. If we have had domestic problems and found
a solution for them what should we do?
     17. What can this accomplish?
     18. How important is the story of how my wife
and I solved our problems?

(P)   19. If we are spiritually fit, we can do what?

     20. People, who do not understand, say things
like what?

(Page 101)
1. What does our experience show us?

(P)   2. What do we do every day?

     3-a. What is wrong with the alcoholic
who can't do that?
          3-b. What is not right?

5-a. What would be his only hope for staying dry?

5-b. Who might mess that up?

7. Would an Al-Anon endorse this last statement?

(P)   8. What is one of our beliefs?

9. What happens when an alcoholic tries to keep away from drinking?

10. Is this a matter of opinion or experience?

11. Why is this so?

(P)   12. So what is our rule?

13. What might that include?

14-a. Would a potential Al-anon be comfortable with this?
14-b. What does our experience demonstrate?

(P)   16. What is the important qualification? (3 sentences)

(Page 102)
1. If we come up with the right answers, what can we do?

2. Do we really have a choice?

3. What two things must we be sure of?

4. What should be our motive if we do go? (2 sentences)

5. If we are uncertain, what should we do instead?

(P)   6a. If we do go, and it is a happy occasion, what should we do?
              6-b. If it is a business opportunity, we should do what?
              8. If a person wants to eat where booze is served, what should
                   we do?
              9. What do we impress upon our friends?

10. Should we tell our friends about our alcoholism?

11. How will they react to the truth?

12. During our drinking days, we were doing what?

13. What are we doing now?

14. What should we not do at this point?

(P)   15-a. What is our job now?
              15-b. We should never hesitate to do
what?
              17. We should never hesitate to do what?

18. If we try to "search out" and "go to" suffering alcoholics, to "carry" this message, what are we promised?

(Page 102 - continued)

(P)   19. Do any of us keep alcohol in our homes?

20. What is the most important reason for doing

so?

21. What do some recovered alcoholics do?

22. How do some feel about liquor in their homes?

23. How do we argue this question?

(Page 103)

1. What position do we take?

(P)   2. What are we very careful to not do?

3. Our experience shows what?

4. What are new members of our Fellowship relieved to learn?

5-a. Intolerance might produce what results?

5-b. Intolerance is classified how?

7. What do drinkers not want to hear?

(P)   8-a. What does our Fellowship hope we might be able to do for the general public?

8-b. What attitude can we not present if we want to be effective?

10. Why is that?

(P)   11. Who made our problems?

12. What were the bottles?

13. What have we stopped doing?

14. Why?

1. Focuses on how the alcoholic's experience, strength and hope can be made to help other alcoholics recover.
2. Also conveys that by helping other alcoholics, we help maintain our recovery.

CHAPTER 10

TO WIVES (104-121)

Now that we have worked the Steps all the way to 12, it is time to learn about How to carry the message. "Having had a spiritual awakening as the result of these steps, we tried to carry this message to alcoholics and practice these principles in all our affairs."

We have received the Promise in our renewed spiritual awakening. We have also received clear cut instructions on how to sponsor others in recovery to support our own recovery. How we get directions in how to apply the principles in all of our affairs.

Alcoholism is a family disease and the wreckage affects the misery of all. This chapter will identify some of the issues that the family surrounding the alcoholic will experience. It also provides suggestions for both the alcoholic and how the alcoholic can mend and compensate the family who also suffered. From this chapter came the Program of Al-Anon.

(Page 104)

(P)   1. Which species of God's kids has this Book referred to, primarily?

2. Who else will it apply to?

3. Is A.A. serving more and more women?

4. Does A.A. work as well for women as it does for men?

(P)   5-a. But for every drinking alcoholic, who else suffers?

5-b. Who will you find in our midst?

(P)   7. The wives, relatives and friends of recovered alcoholics want to do what?

8. Who will this Chapter apply to?

(P)   9. As wives of recovered alcoholics, what do we want others to feel?

10. What do we want to do for others as a beginning point?

11. What feeling do we want to leave you with as you study this Chapter?

(P)   12. Is this Chapter based on ideas and opinions or on experience?

13. What have we lived with?

14. To what two things have we been driven?

(Page 105)

1. What is the everlasting hope of those who love the alcoholic?

(P)   2. Where has our loyalty led us?

3. What are some of these predicaments and attitudes?

(P)   4. What have our homes been like?

5. What happened in the morning?

6-a. What have friends advised us to do?
6-b. What did we do with this advice?

8. What did our men do? What did we do? And then what did they do? (3 sentences)

(P)   9. Why did we not invite friends into our homes?

10. How was our social life?

11. What would happen when we did go out?

(P)   12. How was our financial security?

13. Why was that?

(Page 106)

1. What happened to the checking account?

(P)   2. What was sometimes another serious problem?

3. What was the drinker's excuse for this?

(P)   4. Who interfered with the normal family life?

5. Next day, we did what?

(P)   6. What have we tried to do where the children were concerned?

7. How has the alcoholic reacted?

8. In desperation, what have we done?

9. How did they react to this?

(P)   10. Perhaps we go so far as to what?

11. What did that earn us?

12. But usually we did what?

13. We finally did what?

(P)   14. Did we go to the doctors for help?

15. What prompted this?

(Page 107)

1. Like animals on a treadmill, we did what?

2. Most of us have had to experience what?

3. We sometimes had to witness them going through what?

4. What was often near?

(P)   5. Did we function well under these circumstances?
6. Some were from what?
7. What did we sometimes sense?
8. If we had known the truth, what might we have done?

(P)   9. What could we not understand?

10. We came to believe that they were no longer capable of what?

11. When we came to believe that, what did they do?
12-a. For a while, they would sometimes be what?
12-b. To be followed by what?
14. When we asked why, what would be their answer?

15. It was what?

16. What question did we find ourselves asking?

17. Did we know them when they were on the sauce?

18. What appeared to be the reason they were inaccessible?

(P) 19. If they did love us, how could they not what?

20. What qualities seemed to have vanished?

21. We had to wonder why they couldn't see what?

22. What was so baffling?

(Page 108)

(P) 1. Are these questions very common to those who love alcoholics?

2. What is our hope?

3. Perhaps they have been doing what?

4. What can we see?
      5-a. There may be what?
      5-b. But in most cases, what is the situation?
      5-c. What is the usual reason for this?
   8. What are most of them now that they have recovered?

(P) 9. Try not to do what?

10. Why ?

11. How should you try to treat them?

12. When they blow up, remember what?

(P) 13. Is there an exception?

14. What do we realize?

15. What may an alcoholic of that type try to do?

16. Don't what?

17. If they are of this type what should you do?

18. What should you not let them do?

19. That is especially true when they are aware of what?

(Page 108 - continued)

(P) 20. How many categories does our Basic Text believe alcoholism falls into?

(P) 21. **Category One**: The spouse may be what?

(Page 109)

1. What may be his drinking pattern?

2. Perhaps he does what?

3. How may his drinking affect him?

4. Sometimes he is the source of what?
    5-a. Of what is he positive?
    5-b. That it doesn't do what?

5-c. It is necessary for what?
8. How could you easily insult him?

9. Is he alone in this kind of thinking?

10. What will happen to some of the drinkers?

11. What will happen to many of those who continue to drink?

(P)   12-a. *Category Two:* He may be showing what?
        12-b. How would that be demonstrated?
14. What often happens?
        15-a. What is he willing to admit?
        15-b. But what is it he is sure of?

17. What has he begun to try to do?

18. What may he now be losing?

19. How is his business?

        20-a. Is he at peace with himself?
        20-b. He is becoming aware of what?

        22-a. He sometimes does what?
        22-b. Why does he do this?

        (Page 109 - continued)

        24-a. How is he after a drunk?
        24-b. He will tell you what?

26. But once he has sobered up, what does his mind dwell on?

27. What do we believe about this type of drinker?

28. These are signs of what?

29. Perhaps he can still do what?

30. He hasn't yet done what?

31. What is it we say about a person like this?

(P)   32. **Category Three:** What about this guy?

33. How does he compare to the *Category Two* drinker?

(Page 110)
1-a. What has happened to his friends?
1-b. What is the condition of his home?
1-c. How is he doing with his job?
4. What may be the next scenario?

5. What does he now admit?

6. He clings to what thought?

7. He may have finally arrived at what point?

8. What does his case present?

9. Is this a hopeless case?

(P)   10. **Category Four:** How may you feel about this drinker?

11. Where has he been?

12. How does he act and how does he appear?

13. Coming home from the hospital, what does he do?

14. Perhaps he is so far advanced in the disease that he has experienced what?

15. What do the doctors think you should do with him?

16. Maybe you have had to do what with him?

17. Is this a hopeless situation?

18. How do we know? (2 sentences)

(Page 110 - continued)

For Husband Number One:

(P)   19. What will be difficult?

20. Why is this?

21. Perhaps you, too, enjoy what?

22. Why would that be?

23. How do we know this?

24. What do some but not all of us believe?

(Page 111)

(P)   1. What is the first principle?

2. This should apply even if what?

3. What are most necessary?

(P)   4. What is our next thought?

5. If he thinks you are a nag, what will be the consequences?

6. What two things will probably happen if he considers you a nag?

7. This may well lead to what?

8. He may also do what?

(P)   9. Be determined that drinking will not do what?

10. What will they need?

11. What is possible?

12. Is that based on experience or opinions?

13. What should you not set your heart on?
14. Why?

(P)   15. What do we know?

16. What may he come to appreciate?

17. Where could this lead?

18.   Let him do what?
        (Page - 111 - continued)

19. When he does, you must not be what?

20. Try to do what?

21. Be sure to let him see that you want to be what?

(P)   22-a. When you finally do get into a discussion, what might you do?
           22-b. Or at least read what Chapter in the Big Book?

(Page 112)

1. What might you tell him?

2. Tell him you think he should know more about what subject?

3. What should you show him?

4. What might you say then?

5. By following this approach, you might succeed in doing what?

(P)   6. Very likely, he will have several what?

7. What might you suggest with this possibility?

8. Who do drinkers like to help?

9. What may he then be willing to do?

(P)   10-a. If this doesn't get him talking, what should you do?

     10-b. What will usually happen later?

     12-a. This will require what on your part?
     12-b. But it will what?

14. Meanwhile you might use your time to do what?

15. What might happen if you follow these suggestions?

For Husband Number Two:

(P)   16. What principles should be applied at the start?

17. But after the next binge, you should ask him what?

18. Be sure to not do what?

19. He would want to do this for whom?

(Page - 112 continued)

(P)   20. The chances are what?

21-a. What should you show him?
21-b. What should you tell him?

23. What should you help him understand?

24. What do you tell him you found interesting?

25. If he is shy about the solution, ask him to read what Chapter?

(Page 113)
1. What may this do for him?

(P)   2. Your cooperation will mean a lot if he is what?

3. If he is not really interested, what should you do?

4. What should you not do?

5. What have you accomplished?

6. He now knows what very important fact?

7. What should you never do?

8. Sooner or later, you very likely will see him doing what?

9-a. What should you wait for?
9-b. Why should you wait?

Now for Husband Number Three:
(P)   11. What may be the case here?

12. If you are sure he wants to stop drinking, what can you do?

13-a. He may not be what?

13-b. But he is reasonably sure to do what?

13-c. If he does, what will probably happen?

16. If he doesn't go for the program immediately, what will probably be the case?

17. What should you not do?

18. Let him do what?

19. Remain cheerful as he does what?

20. When should you mention this topic?

21. What might be a better approach?

22. What can they sometimes do?

(Page 113 - continued)

23. If your husband is otherwise a normal person what might you hope for?

Now for Husband Number Four:

24. Are alcoholics at this stage hopeless?

25. Were many recovered alcoholics at this point?

26. What had everybody done?

27. What seemed certain?

28. Yet, they experienced what?

(P)   1. Is that true for all of them?

2. What is one reason for an exception?

3. What is another reason?

4. Who can determine if these situations are present?

5. In any event, what should you do?

6. How may he react?

7-a. If he is in an institution and serious about this Program, what might you do?

7-b. When should you possibly not do this?

9. Is this recommendation a sound one?

10. What is it based on?

11. Since this Book was published, what has happened?

12. What has been A.A.'s experience with most of them?

13. From whence comes this miracle?

(P)   14. On the other hand, you may have an alcoholic who should be what?

15. What is the truth for some alcoholics?

16-a. If they become too dangerous what should you do?

16-b. Who can help you with this decision?

18-a. When this level of alcoholism is present, who suffers?

18-b. But not more than whom?

(P)   20. Sometimes you may have to do what?

21. Is this based on opinions or experience?

22. What will make such an event easier?

(P)   23. If you have a drinking alcoholic on your hands, you probably worry about what?

24. Why do you become more withdrawn?

25. What subject do you not care to talk about with anyone?

(Page 115)

1. What can you tell the children?

2. When his drinking is really bad, what do you do?

(P)   3. What have we found?

4. What can you let your friends know?

5. Be very careful not to do what?

(P)   6. What will happen when you have told your friends the truth?

7. What will happen to the barriers you have created?

8. You will no longer feel what?

9. Is the alcoholic normally a weak character?

10. What will do wonders for you?

(P)   11. What should you use in dealing with the children?

12. Unless Dad is physical with the children, what is it best not to do?
13. What should you do?

14. If you do that, what will very likely happen?

(P)   15. What have you felt obliged to do?

16. What should you do instead?

17. What is the best thing to do?
18-a. Although you want to protect him, what should you not do?
18-b. Why?

20. Discuss what with him?
(Page 116)

1. What should you ask him?

2. Be careful to not do what?

(P)   3. What is another terrible fear? (2 sentences)

4. May this happen?

5. Or is this old hat by now?

6. If it happens again, what might you do?

7. What could losing his job prove to be?

8. What might it do for the drinker?

9. What is it you now know?
10-a. What has this proved to be for many of us?

10-b. Why was that so and where did it

lead us?

(P)   12. What remark have we seen before?

13. If God can solve the problems of alcoholism, what else can He do?

14. What have we wives found?

15. As our husbands recovered, what did we see?

(P)   16. At first, what did many of us believe?

17. How did we think of ourselves?

18. What silly idea did we have?

19. What is it we try to do now?
20-a. What happens when we do?
20-b. What is one of the wonderful things about it?

(Page 117)
1-a. What do we urge you to do?
1-b. Why do we?
1-c. What is the source of this change of attitude?
4. Should you join you husband in this journey?

(P)   5. What is going to make you very happy?

6. Will this be the end of difficult times?

7. Where are we on this journey of recovery?

8. In spite of the happiness, what can be expected?

9. Why is this?

10. Is this the way it should be?

(P)   11. What now will be put to the test?

12-a. How should these disagreements be regarded?

12-b. Why would we view them in that light?

14. Will the mistakes you make bring an end to your efforts?

15. Instead, how will we view them?

16. What will emerge as you persevere?

(P)   17. What are some snags you will encounter?

18-a. How will your hubby be on occasions?

18-b. How will you be tempted to respond?

20. If you do, where may it lead?

(Page - 117 - continued)
21-a. What are these dissensions within the family?

21-b. Especially to whom?

23. In troubled times, what must you do?

24. What can you never forget?

25. Do you always have to give into him because of this?

26. Just be careful to not do what?

(Page 118)

(P)   1. What will you both find?

2. The next time the two of you get into it, what should one
of you say?

3. If your husband is serious about his recovery, he will do what?

(P)   4. What is it your husband knows?

5. What does he want to do?

6. You shouldn't do what?

7. What is his initial problem?
8. What are the watchwords?

9. If you have learned to demonstrate these to him, what will you receive back from him?
10. What slogan is quoted here?

11. If each of you is applying the Steps to your individual lives, what will be the result?

(P)   12. What do we women carry?

13. Once he has recovered, what is it natural to feel?

14-a. Are the chances pretty good that he will become
"Mr. Wonderful" overnight?
14-b. Why is that?

16. You must try to be what?

(P)   17. What is another hurdle you might encounter?

18. What thought may really bother us?

19. When we entertain those thoughts, what is it we have forgotten?

20. What will your husband be the first to say?

(Page 119)

1. Without you, what would have happened to him?

2. When these thoughts occur, try to replace them with what?

3. After all, what has taken place?

(P) 4. What is still another difficulty you may face?

5-a. What have you been starving for?

5-b. Yet, what does the fool do?

7. You think he should be doing what?

8. What fact should you remember?

9. What will happen sometimes?

10. Who will you find hanging out in your home?

11. Will they all be likable?

12. What does he do for them that he won't do for you?

13. Is it a good idea to straighten him out on this?

14. What would be a big mistake?

15. Instead, what should you do?

16. What do we suggest you do?

17. What do they need?

(P) 18. What is probably true?

19. Therefore, you probably need what?

20. If you cooperate with, rather than complain at him, what will happen?

21.   Both of you will awaken to a new what?
(Page 120)
1. What should both of you think about?

2. If you do, what will be inevitable?

3. What will you give up and what will you get?

(P)   4. Perhaps you will encounter what as a real disappointment?

5. If you know he really wants to recover, should you be worried?
6-a. What is infinitely better?
6-b. But a relapse may not be what?
8. A relapse may do what for him?

9-a. What will you not need to remind him of?
9-b. Why won't you need to do that?
11. What should you do instead?

(P)   12. What will place your husband's recovery in jeopardy?

13. If he is at a weak moment, what might happen if you do?

(P)   14. What is it we never try to do?

15.   What will he notice very quickly?

16. Are you supposed to give him complete freedom?

17. Why?

18. What if he gets drunk?

19. God either has or hasn't done what?

20. When do you need to know this?

21. Then the two of you can do what?

22. If return to drinking is to be prevented, what must happen?

(Page 121)

(P)   1. What do we realize?

2. What may we have seemed to do?
                3-a. If it appears to be so with you, please accept our what?
                3-b. How do we like to be lectured?
5. What has this Chapter been based on?

6. How did we learn?

7. So what is the main motivation for this Chapter?

(P)   8. Our message to you potential members is what?

MAIN POINTS

1. This chapter sheds light on how wives can adopt the principles of the Steps to help them deal with an alcoholic. These ideas later become Al-Anon in 1952
2. This chapter gives practical remedies from the wives of early AA member pioneers. It helps wives understand the problems faced with an alcoholic husband, including

circumstances like whether divorce or separation are desirable.

CHAPTER 11

THE FAMILY AFTERWARD (122-135)

This chapter is for the entire family. We learned that just because the drinking ends, all the ramifications and underlying problems do not. In "The Family Afterward" we see how each family member can apply the Twelve Steps to family life to return peace, harmony and love to the entire family.

(Page 122)

(P)   1. Our women folk have suggested what?

2. What impression may they have created?

3. Successful adjustment means what?

4. All members should do what?
5. What process is involved?

6. Which members of the family will very likely have some fixed ideas?
7. What is it each one wants?

8. What have we found?

9. The product of this is what?

(P)   10. Each one wants to play what?

11. Each is trying to do what?

12. He unconsciously is trying to do what?

(P)   13. Cessation of drinking is what?

14. What did a doctor have to say about this?

15. What should families realize?

16. Each may what?

(Page 123)
1-a. What may appear to be alluring?
1-b. Where may they lead us?

(P)   3. What two things will the authors of this Book tell us as we begin the study of this Chapter?
4. What does the family long for?

5. What do they remember?
6-a. How do they view life today?
6-b. What problem does that present?

(P)   8. Now that dad is sober, how do members of the family feel?

9. What do they expect?

10. What do they sometimes demand?

11. Who do they believe owes them a speedy return to the good old days?
12-a. What has been coming apart for years?
12-b. They are now what?
14. What will it take?
15-a. What will ultimately happen?

15-b. How soon may it happen?

(P)   17-a. What does father know?
              17-b. What may be required for financial
recovery?

              17-c. He shouldn't be what?

    20. Will he someday be financially well off?

    21. What will the wise family do?

(P)   22. With what will the family be plagued from
time to time?

    23. What will be the first impulse when these
appear?

    24. With what may the family be possessed?
              (Page 124)
          1-a. What do we think about this?
          1-b. And in direct conflict with what?

(P)   3. What did Henry Ford once say?

    4. When is that true?

    5. What is it we do to grow?

    6. What does the alcoholic's past prove to be?

(P)   7. Our painful past may prove to be what?

    8. When the family is in recovery, what do we
think they should be willing to do?
        9. What does working with others prove to be?
          10-a. What thought must we hang onto?
          10-b. It will be the key to what?
      12. What can happen as we share our past?
(P)   13. Will digging up some parts of our past prove
harmful?

14. What example are we given?

15. In the beginning of their recovery, how did it go?

16. What was in view?

17. Then, because of some trifling event, what happened?

18. A few of us have had what?

(Page 125)
1. What have some husbands and wives been forced to do?

2. In most cases, how did the alcoholic fare?

3. So, unless there is a good reason, what do we think should not happen?

(P)   4. What do families of Alcoholics Anonymous not keep?

5. Everyone in their group knows what?

6. In ordinary life, what would this produce?

7. What is rare among us?
8-a. Who is it we do talk about a great deal?
8-b. But in what spirit does this take place?

(P)   10. What is another principle we carefully observe?

11. We find it better to do what?

12-a. What can a person do to himself?
12-b. What would be the effect if it came

from someone else?

14-a. Family members should be very careful to do what?
14-b. Why is that?

16. Alcoholics are what?

17. Do we grow out of it quickly?

(P)   18. Many alcoholics are what?

19. To what do they run?

20. At the beginning of recovery, what will happen?
21-a. He will plunge into what?

(Page 126)
1-b. What is the other path he may plunge into?
2. In either case, what is reasonably certain?

3. How do we know?

(P)   4. What do we believe to be dangerous?
5-a. Initially, what will be the family's attitude?
5-b. But then what will happen?

7. If dad throws himself into business, how will he be?

8-a. Who may he neglect?
8-b. When this is pointed out to him, how will he react?

10. If he is not irritable, how will he appear?

11. What may mother do?
12-a. The whole family is what?

12-b. What do they do about it?

14. At the start of such criticism, what is happening?

15. What is the alcoholic doing?

16. He is trying very hard to do what?

(P)   17. Sometimes, the family does what?

18. Since they have been so neglected, what do they think they deserve?

19. What do they want from him?

20. What do they expect him to give them?

21. But what does dad do?

22. What happens?
        (Page 126 - continued)

23. How does he react?

24. Sometimes he will do what?

25. How well does the family understand?

26. What do they do at this point?

(P)   27. This sort of thing can be what?

28. Who is at fault?

29. If they continue to argue, what will happen?

(Page 127)
1. What must the family realize?

2. For what should they be thankful?

3. What else should they do?

4. What should they remember?
     5-a. If they can see the reality of things, they will not take what so seriously?
     5-b. When will this change?

(P)   7. What should the head of the house remember?

8. What will he probably never be able to do?

9. What danger must he consider?

10. Even though financial recovery is progressing, what do we know?

11. For us, what must come first?

(P)   12-a. What has suffered more than anything else?
     12-b. What should the alcoholic do?
    14. If he really wants to recover, what should he do?
     15-a. We know that some alcoholics are faced with what?
     15-b. But the alcoholic must remember what?

(P)   17. What will happen when each member of the family begins to apply his respective Twelve Step Program?

18. These family meetings will work if they are conducted without what?
     19-a. Little by little, the family will do what?
     19-b. And father will begin to do what?
     (Page 128)

1. What very important thing becomes our guiding principle?

(P) 2. Rather than get caught up in business, assume father has had what?

3. What happens overnight?

4. He becomes a what?

5. He can't do what?
6. As soon as the family can accept his sobriety, they begin to do what?
7. He talks only of what?

8. He may do which of two things?

9. What may he tell his wife?

(P) 10. What happens when father goes religious?

11. Who may they become jealous of?

12. Even though they are happy he is sober, what may they not like?

13. What may they have forgotten?

14. They may not be able to see what?

15. Dad really isn't what, they think?
16. If he really wants to make amends to the family, why is he doing what?
17. Since he is too busy to take care of them, who does he tell them will?
18. What do they think has happened to dad?

(P) 19. He really isn't what?

20. What have most of us experienced?

21. What have we indulged in?

22. Who can we be compared to?

23. What knows no bounds?

(Page 129)
1. What does father feel he has found?

2. What will he do initially?
        3-a. What may he not be able to see for a while?
        3-b. Which will continue to pay off only so long as he does what?

(P)   5. What will happen when the family cooperates.?

        6-a. What will he finally discover?
        6-b. What has been missing?

     8   When the family realizes the truth, what will happen?

     9. With an understanding family, what usually happens?

(P)   10. The opposite will happen if the family does what?

        11-a. Dad will recognize what?
        11-b. But now he sees himself how?

    13. If the family doesn't let up, what will happen?

    14. Instead of becoming a member of the family again, what usually happens?

(P)   15-a. What does the family need not do?
        15-b. They should do what, however?

17-a. Even if he does what?
17-b. It is a good idea to let him do what?

19. In the early part of his sobriety, is his activity really important?

20-a. How do some of his actions appear?

(Page 130)
1-b. We believe he will ultimately be on a firmer foundation than who?
2. He will be less likely to do what?

(P)   3. What have those of us who have gone spiritually balmy finally done?
4-a. What has our dream world been replaced with?
4-b. It was accompanied by what?
6. What have we come to believe?

7. Why is this?

8.   What are these for us?

9. We have found no incompatibility between what two aspects of our lives?

(P)   10. What is another suggestion?
11-a. What will they find hard to disapprove of?
11-b. Even though the alcoholic may do what?
13. What has proved to be a great help to the alcoholic?

(P)   14. In what other area will there be changes?

15. While dad was drinking, what was mother

becoming?

16. How did she do?

17. Because of drinking, she was forced to do what?

18.   Even when he tried, what would happen?

(Page 131)

1. What did mother do?

2. When would father do what he was told?

3. By default, mother became what?

4. Now that dad is sober, what will he attempt to do?

5. This could lead to trouble unless they do what?

(P)   6. Drinking isolates what from what?

7. Father may have abandoned what other part of his life while drinking?
8. When he gets involved in these things again, what might happen?

9. What may the family feel?

10. Instead of getting back into normal activities, the family may do what?

(P)   11. In the early days of sobriety, the mother and father should do what?

12. What will father find it necessary to do?

13. What kind of new acquaintances might be made?

14. What about the community in which they live?

15. What about the possibility of joining a religious body?

(P)   16. Could this prove to be helpful?

17-a. Now that the alcoholic has recovered, what may he find?

(Page 132)
1-b. Will he now agree with religious folks, without question?
2. If he does not engage in debate on religious matters, what will happen?
3. What can he and his family prove to be?
4. Surprisingly enough, to whom may he bring new hope?
5. What is the intent of the foregoing?
6. What is our attitude on this matter?
7. With what religious body are we affiliated?
8. What should guide each individual in this matter?

(P)   9. What have we been speaking of so far?
10. Specifically, we have been dealing with what?
11. But we sure aren't what?
12. What would happen to newcomers if they didn't see the fun we have?
13. What is it we really insist on?

14-a. We try not to indulge in pessimism over what?

14-b. Nor do we try to shoulder what?

16. When we see a suffering alcoholic, what do we do?

17. For his benefit, what do we do?

18. But what do we not do?

(P) 19. What do we think is useful?

20. How do some outsiders react to our stories?

21. We should be able to do what?

22. Why is this?

(P) 23. Everybody knows one thing. What is it?

24. So, what should each family do?

(Page 133)

1. Of what are we sure?

2. We cannot subscribe to what?

3. What is now clear?

4. To some of us, it came as a surprise to learn what?

5-a. What are we to avoid?

5-b. But if it does come, how do we treat it?

(P) 7. What about a body that has been badly abused by drinking?

8. Of what are we convinced?

9. What are recovered alcoholics?

10. What have we seen?

11. Recovered alcoholics rarely display what?

(P)   12. But this does not mean what?

13. We have an abundance of what?

14. We should not hesitate to do what?

15. Most of them, in the past, would do what?

16. What should we remember not to do?

17. What do we find their services to be?

(P)   18. What did one doctor have to say about this Book?

19. What did he think all alcoholics should have available?
                    (Page 134)
        1. Why did he suggest this?

2. What have many of us noticed?

(P)   3. Now about what?

4. What does alcohol do to the sexual appetite of some?

5. In early sobriety, what may some of us encounter?

6. May this be an upsetting situation?

7. Some who experienced this later found what?

8. Whom should we not hesitate to consult?

9. Is this condition usually permanent?

(P)   10. How may things go with the children?

11. Why may that be?

12. Even though they don't say it, how may they feel?

13. By what are some children dominated?

14. What is it they may have trouble doing?

15. Will this attitude change rapidly?

(P)   16. What will they see in time?

17-a. When this begins to happen, what is a good idea?

17-b. What will probably happen then?

19. What kind of results can be expected?

(Page 135)

(P)   1. What must the alcoholic do, regardless of what others do?

2. Of what must they be convinced?

3. What will it take to make believers of them?

(P)   4. What example are we given here?

5. What other faults did this alcoholic have?

6. What did his wife have to say about this?

7. What was his response?

8. What did his wife continue to do?

9. What did he do to get even with her?

(P)   10. Was this the wrong thing to do?

11. What did he do about it?

12-a. Although he recovered, what did he do?

12-b. Would it appear his wife may have adopted the Al-Anon way of life?

14. What was she able to see?

(P)   15. What three mottoes are given here?

MAIN POINTS

1. This chapter focuses on the entire family and how the impact of the alcoholic has affected it.
2. In a way the entire family has taken on some of the sickness.
3. Offers way for the family to recover.
4. Secrets are to be avoided whenever possible.
5. Helps the family to understand the disease of addiction and that the alcoholic is sick beyond human aid and needs God.
6. There is also a theme of how the recovered alcoholic can be "happy, joyous and free".

CHAPTER 12

TO EMPLOYERS (136-150)

This chapter is for the alcoholic in recovery at the workplace. Any business will have a number of employees what are active alcoholics. We are not alone. In fact, many employers are in recovery as well, or know about it enough to understand that recovering alcoholics can be great workers and assets.

This is the only chapter that was not written by Bill W. Hank P, a terminated executive of a large corporation authored it and tells his story as an introduction. In the chapter, "The Doctor's Opinion" Dr. Silkworth tells of the alcoholic who thought his case so hopeless that he had gone to a deserted barn to die. That hopeless alcoholic was Hank P. His story, "The Unbeliever," can be found in the First Edition of the Big Book.

(Page 136)

(P)   1. To begin this Chapter, we are going to focus on whom?

2. Does he have extensive experience in placing and displacing employees?

3. From what viewpoint does he view alcoholics?

4. His views should prove helpful to whom?

(P)   5. What was my position?

6. One day my secretary informed me of what?

7. My reply was?

8. Of what had I warned this man?

9. What happened not long after the warning?

10. As the result, what did I tell him?

(P)   11. My secretary informed me that it was who?

12. While I expected to hear some begging for the old job, I was surprised to hear the brother say what? (rest of paragraph)

(P)   13. Another time, when I opened a letter, what fell out?

(Page 137)
1. What was the newspaper clipping?

2. After a drinking binge, what had he done?

3. What had I done to him shortly before?

(P)   4. In still another experience, I heard from whom?

5. What was the purpose of her call?

6. Why was she interested in knowing the answer to her question?

7. What had been my experience with him?

(P)   8. What is one reason these men died?

9. What was the irony of all this?

10. What saved me from joining the three who had gone on before?
11-a. What had my alcoholism cost my employer?
11-b. Why is that?
13. Is this kind of thing uncommon?

14. What does our experience lead us to believe?

(P)   15. What does almost every responsible employer feel?

16. Have employers always treated alcoholics fairly?

17. To many employers, what does the alcoholic appear to be?

18. If an employee had special talents or was a "fair-haired boy," what would the employer sometimes do?

19. What have some employers tried?

20. Once in awhile, there was a lack of what?

(Page 138)

1. Looking back at the time we were drinking, what can we now say?

(P)   2. An example is that of an officer of a large bank who knows what?

3. What did this officer share with the author?

4. It looked like an opportunity to help so I did what?

5. What was his comment?

(P)   6. I had only one answer and it was what?

7. What did I ask for?

8. What good might that do?

9. What did I point out to the executive?

10. What did I then ask?

11. The man's reply was what?

(P)   12. What did I do then and why?

13. What was he unable to believe?

(Page 139)
1. What was my only choice?

(P)   2. What did happen to the man?
3. Did he have much difficulty accepting our program?
4. He is on the road to what?
5. What two important things did this illustrate?

(P)   6. For the employer who wants to help, what is the first thing he should do?
7. Regardless of what type of drinker you are, your thinking may well be what?
8. What type of drinker is usually most annoyed with the alcoholic?

9. The moderate drinker understands his reaction to alcohol that will produce some fixed ideas that are what for the alcoholic?

10. What can the moderate drinker do?

11. How does the moderate drinker handle his drinking?

12. On a given evening, the moderate drinker can drink to excess and do what the next morning?

13. What is liquor to the moderate drinker?

14. What is the moderate drinker unable to see?

(P)   15. When moderate drinkers deal with alcoholics, there is a natural reaction to feel that the alcoholic is what?

16. Will this get better as the moderate drinker has a better understanding of alcoholism?

(P)   17. How will it strike you as you look at an alcoholic in your organization?

18. What qualities would you normally find?

19. When he is sober, how does he perform?

(Page 140)
1. If he didn't drink, what would he be worth?

2. How about other sick employees?

3. What question must be answered?

4. If the answer is "yes," then what do we have for the employer?

(P)   5. First, what question must be answered?
         6-a. If the question is difficult to answer, what should the employer do?

6-b. Why might that help?

8. As a businessman, what should come first?

9. If he can concede that the person is sick, what is the next step?

10. How should his past be considered?

11. Can you accept the reality of the victim of alcoholism?

(P)   12. What information coming from a doctor shocked Hank?

13. What could that explain?

14. How are normal drinkers affected?

(P)   15. What has your man probably been trying to do?

16. Some may even be what?

17. What may you be at a loss to understand?

18. To what can these incidents be attributed?

19. When under the influence, what will an alcoholic sometimes do?

(Page 141)
1. Afterward, how will he be?

2. Most of the time, these incidents are what?

(P)   3. This is not to say what?

4. What may this kind of person do?

5. What will some people do when they see you trying to help them?

6. If you believe he is not sincere in his desire to quit drinking, you should do what?
7. What is it you are not doing for him?

8. Losing his job may prove to be what?

9. What may it give him?

10. What did the author know about himself as long as he had a job?

11. What action could his employer have taken that might have made a big difference in his life?

(P)   12. But what about the ones who really want to stop drinking?
13. What can pay dividends for them?

(P)   14. Maybe you already have what?

15. What may you both want?

16. What do you now know?

17. What are you now willing to do?

(P)   18. To make your initial approach what can you tell him you know?

19-a. You might also say you appreciate his what?

19-b. Also, you would like to do what?
19-c. But under what condition?

(Page 142)
1. What sort of an attitude is best?

(P)   2. Next, of what do you assure him?

3. What should you express to him?

4. At this point, what might you do?
     5-a. Tell him you believe he is what?
     5-b. What question do you ask him?

7. Why would you ask this question?

8. What question must be answered before you proceed?

9. You should be assured he is willing to do what?

(P)   10. If he says, "yes", can you be sure of his sincerity?

11. What should he be thoroughly probed on?

12. Of what do you need to be satisfied?

(P)   13. What is a matter for your discretion?

14-a. If he decides to quit for a little while, believing he can then drink successfully, you should probably do what after his next binge?
14-b. By then, you can be reasonably certain that he is what?

16. What should he understand before the conversation is concluded?

17. What do you need to find out about this person?

18. If he is not sincere, you may decide to do what?

19. Would this be too severe?

(P)   20. Once you are convinced he is sincere, what

might you do?

21. If he is drinking or coming off a drunk, what may he need?

(Page 143)

1. Who should make that call regarding physical treatment?

2. Why may this be necessary?

3. Should this process be either long or expensive?

4. Why is this desirable?

5-a. If this is indicated, you may find it necessary to help him in what way?
5-b. But what should the alcoholic clearly understand?

7. Why is that?

(P)   8. If the man agrees to proceed, what must he be told?

9. What should he understand?

10. What must happen to him if he is to survive alcoholism?

11. Where must we place recovery in our priorities?

(P)   12. With what question are you faced?

13. What questions should you be able to

answer?

14. What might you do with him to help answer these questions?

(P)   15. But what about the subject matter of this Book?

(Page 144)
1. How may some of our ideas appear?

2. Perhaps you might not agree with what?
        3-a. Do we believe we have the only solution?

        3-b. Why do we believe in it?
    5.   What are you really interested in?

6. Whether or not your employee likes our program, what will result anyway?

7. Will this prove harmful to him?

(P)   8. What do we now suggest you do?

        9-a. When is the best time for your man to read this book?
        9-b. What may be the result?

(P)   11. What do we hope the doctor will do?

12. When the man receives this book, it is best to not do what?

13. What must the man do?

(P)   14. What are you betting on?

15. Is that a sure thing?

16. If you persist, what will happen to your odds?

17. As our work spreads and our numbers increase, what is our hope?

18. Meanwhile, of what are we sure?

(P)   19. When your man returns, what should you do first?

20. What do you want to know?

21. If he believes he has your confidence, what can you expect?
                    (Page 145)
(P)   1. Do you think you can remain composed as he shares his story with you?
        2. What may he reveal to you?

3. In fact, you should be prepared for what?

4. What might you consider doing about this?

5. How might you handle the money situation?

(P)   6. Where might you be able to offer some direction?

7. Will you be willing to let him be completely open with you, provided he doesn't do what?

8. What will such an attitude on your part buy you?

(P)   9. What are alcoholics greatest enemies?

10. What is true in any business that hires a number of employees?

11. Being the sensitive people that alcoholics are, how might we view some of the normal infighting?

12. Is this always true?

13. What may be used against us?

(P)   14. What situation is recalled?

15. Would this be classified as gossip?

16. What is another case?

17. Was this kept confidential?

18. What effect will this have on the alcoholic's chances?

(Page 146)
1. Many times, the employer can do what?
2-a. He cannot do what?
2-b. But what can he do?

(P)   4. Generally speaking, what are alcoholics?

5. How do they live their lives?

6. It will be in his character to do what?

7. With the body still recovering, how may he approach his task?

8. What may you have to do?

9. What may you need to encourage him to do?

10. What may he wish to do?

11. How should you respond to this?

12. Why should you be considerate of this activity?

(P)   13-a. After a few months of recovery, how

else may you find him useful to you?
13-b. Provided what condition exists?

15. What unique situation will you find here?

16. As the result of his spiritual way of life, he will never do what?

(P)	17. How can you view your man?

18. What might make you suspicious?

19. What might you believe the next time his wife calls?

20-a. If he has been drinking and is serious about recovery, what	will he tell you?
20-b. Even if he is faced with what?

22. Of what is he certain?

23. What will he appreciate?

(Page 147)
1. If he is truly on our Program, what can he do?

(P)	2. What must you decide if he returns to drinking?

3. If you have any doubts regarding his sincerity, what should you do?

4. If you are convinced he is really trying, what might you do?

5. Since you have met your commitment to him, what may you do with a clear conscience?

(P)	6. Is there something else you might do?

7. Who else might benefit from this Book?

8. What message do you want to pass along to them?

9. Where do junior executives find themselves sometimes?

10. Often, the men who work under them prove to be what else?

11. Therefore, the junior exec might be tempted to do what?

12. In what situation may they be placing themselves?

(P)   13. After the junior exec has read this Book, what may he be able to do?
14. You are putting me in a what?

15. I have learned something about what?

16. I must tell you that if you are an alcoholic you might be what?

17. What does the firm want to do?

18-a. What will we be willing to do, if you are willing to try this program?
(Page 148)

1-b. We will keep what confidential?

2. But if you want to keep on drinking, you had better do what?

(P)   3. What may your junior exec not agree with?

4. What should he maybe not do?

5. But what may he have learned?

6. It will enable him to treat the employee how?

7. From what will it free him?

(P)   8. What does this boil down to?

9. If he wants to stop drinking, what should he be given?

10. If that is not the case, what should you do?

11. Exceptions to this rule are what?

(P)   12. We think this approach will do what?

13. First, it will permit what?

14. At the same time, you will find what other benefit?

15. What might alcoholism be doing to your business?

16. What do we hope our suggestions will do for you?

17. We believe we are being sensible in doing what?

(P)   18. What happened the other day?

19. Even though the vice president was presented with information that could profit their company greatly, what was his response?

(Page 149)
1. What does this company do with some of its money?

2. Are they concerned with the cost of doing

business?

3. What benefits have they provided their employees?

4. Do they display a real interest in their workers?

5. Of what do they believe they are free?

(P)   6. How may this attitude be classified?

7. What is our inward feeling toward these views?

8. At what would he very likely be shocked to learn?

9. What may be true about their payroll?

10. What knowledge may top executives be lacking?

11. Even for those certain they have no problem drinkers on hand, what might prove to be profitable?
12. What may you find?

(P)   13. Who does this Chapter refer to?

14. What sort of person was the vice president thinking of?
15-a. How would his personnel policy apply to them?
15-b. What is he unable to distinguish between?

(P)   17. The alcoholic employee should not receive what?

18. He should not be what?

19. How will recovered alcoholics respond to this type of treatment?

20. He will not do what?

21. What will he do instead?

(P)   22. Today, I own what?
                    (Page 150)

1-a. How many employees do I have?
1-b. But what do they do?

3. Why would they do that? (2 sentences)

4. What have I enjoyed?

MAIN POINTS

1. Alcoholics can be valuable employees when working the Program of AA.
2. Alcoholics in recovery are often the best workers because of the Twelve Steps.

CHAPTER 13

A VISION FOR YOU (151-164)

"A Vision For You" is an amazing piece of writing that provides hope and guidance for alcoholics through Alcoholics Anonymous. Like the rest of the Big Book, it is full of experience and combined with spirituality.

"Have had a spiritual awakening as the result of these steps", is a poignant piece that captures the essence of Alcoholics Anonymous. It tells us that as a part of our recovery, to ensure it, we find it necessary to find other alcoholics who are suffering as we once were. This allows us to let them know that we understand the misery, yet we have found healing. We explain our experience, strength and hope and are a demonstration of the Higher Power (God) we found through our Program. If we find that they want what we have, we give them a copy of the Big Book and show them where the good meeting are that we attend to share the road to happy destiny.

(Page 151)

(P)   1. What is drinking for most folks?

2. It is release from what?

3. What else is it for most people?

4.   How about us?

5. What is gone?

6. What are the good old days?

7. When will we be able to recapture those moments?
8-a. What did we yearn for?
8-b. With what were we obsessed?
10. What was the truth?

(P)   11. As people became less tolerant of us, what did we do?

12. As we became citizens of King Alcohol, shivering inhabitants
    of   his mad world, what did we experience?

13. It did what and became what?
14-a. What did some of us seek?
14-b. What were we hoping to find?

16-a. What success did we have?
16-b. This would be followed by what?
16-c. What did we face?

19. Who will have no trouble understanding what we have just covered?

(P)   20. Once in awhile, what may a dried out serious drinker say?
         (4 sentences)

      21. As ex-problem drinkers, how do we react to such
         declarations?
                     (Page 152)
         1. He is like who?

      2. What is he doing to himself?

      3. What is it he really wants to do?
            4-a. Soon, what will he do?
            4-b. Why?
         6. What can he not see?

      7. Someday, what will he be unable to imagine?

      8. What will he then come to know as few people can?

      9. Where will he be?

      10. For what will he wish?

(P)   11. What have we shown?

      12. You might say what?

(P)   13. What do we have?

      14. What is it called?

15. What will you find there?

16. How will it effect your imagination?

17. How will you feel about being alive?

18. What are your future years promised to be?

19. Where will we find this?

(P)   20. What questions do you have?

(Page 152 - continued)

(P)   21. Where do we say you will find them?

22. Who will you find near you?

23. How many if you live in a large city?

24. Where will they come from?

25. What will they become to you?

26-a. How will you be bound to them?

26-b. Why will that be so?
26-c. And, together, you will begin what?

1. You will then know what?

2. You will then learn the full meaning of what?

(P)   3. What may seem incredible?

4. What question will arise?

5. What is the practical answer?

      6-a. How should you wish for them?

      6-b. What should you be willing to do?

      6-c. Of what are we certain?

9. What still exhibits itself among us?

10. What proof is there of that statement?

(P)   11. What is our hope?

12. Of what are we sure?

      13-a. They will then do what?

      13-b. What will be the result of these actions?

(P)   15. What did you learn in "Chapter 7?"

16. Since you followed the directions laid out for us in that Chapter, what has happened?

17. What will you now want to know?

18. How do we propose to give you a

glimpse of what can be your   future?

(P)   19-a. The brief account begins when?
            19-b. How did it begin?

21. How did his business deal go?

22. If his business deal had gone off well,
what would have been his expected future?
(Page 154)

1. But how did his deal wind up?

2. What did the proceeding produce?

(P)   3. Very discouraged, how did he find
himself?

4-a. In what physical condition was
he?

4-b. How long had he been sober?
4-c. What could he see for himself?
7. What was it he really wanted?

(P)   8. On that afternoon, what was he
wondering?

9. What was at one end of the lobby?

10. What was at the other end?

11. What did he see in there?

12. What might he find in there?

13-a. Without a couple of drinks he
was afraid he would not
have what?
13-b. How would his weekend be?

(P)   15. Even though he knew he couldn't afford to drink, what was he thinking?

16. Why not? He had been sober how long?

17. What did his alcoholic mind (the insidious insanity) say to
       him?

18. What did he experience with that thought?

19. How secure did he feel?

20. What was he experiencing?

21. What did he do?

22. What was he still hearing?
       (Page 154 - continued)

(P)   23-a. Who did he think of?
           23-b. Especially who did he think of?

25. Should it be very difficult to find one?

26. What would he do?

27. What returned and what did he do because it did?

(Page 155)

1. What did he do then?

(P)   2-a. Where did his call lead him?
          2-b. In what condition was this
formerly able and respected person?
          4. What was his situation?
              5-a. What was his desperate desire?
              5-b. Had he given up hope?
          7. He knew he was not normal but what
was it he did not know?

(P)   8. After Bill told his story, with what did
Dr. Bob agree?

          9-a. What did Dr. Bob concede as
being absolutely
              necessary?
          9-b. How did he first feel about the
Program of action?

     11. What did he admit to Bill?

     12. What had Dr. Bob rationalized?

          13-a. What was his argument?
          13-b. The result of which would bring
more suffering to whom?

     15. To what length was he not willing to
go?

(P)   16. Being intrigued, what did Dr. Bob and

Anne do?

17. Three weeks later, what did Dr. Bob do?

18. Was this just an overnight drunk?

19-a. What did it convince Dr. Bob he must do?

(Page 156)

1-b. If he wanted God to do what?

(P)   2. What did Dr. Bob do one morning?

3. He surprised to learn what two things?

4. He got into his car and did what?

5. Why did he tremble as he made his amends?

(P)   6-a. When did he finally come home?
             6-b. What shape was he in?

8. How well did it work for him?
Dr. Bob had his last drink on the morning of June 10, 1935. He lived the rest of his life sober and passed away November 16,1950.

9. The major liabilities resulting from 30 years of hard drinking were repaired in how many years?

Dr. Bob had his last drink in June, 1935, and this Book was published in April, 1939.

(P)   10. Was life easy and comfortable for these two men?

11. What did they have plenty of?

12. What did both of them realize they must do?

13. So, what did Dr. Bob do one day? *Comment: The date was June 11, 1935. The day following Dr. Bob's last drink.*

14. He explained their need and asked what?

(Page 156 - continued)

(P)   15. What was the nurse's reply?

16. What shape was the prospect in at the time of the call?
(the rest of paragraph)

Comment: Notice (*) referring to the footnote regarding Bill & Dr. Bob's 12th Step call on Bill D.

(P)   17. What did they think of their chances of success with this guy?

18. What was not well understood at that time?

(Page 157)

1. What did Dr. Bob ask the nurse to do? (2 sentences)

(P)   2. What happened two days later?

3. What did Bill D. ask Bill & Dr. Bob? (2 sentences)

(P)   4. How did they answer him?

(P)   5. What was written on his face?
6. Did Bill D. believe there could be any hope for him?
(the rest of paragraph)

(P)   7. What happened over the next hour?
8. What was Bill D.'s response? (3 sentences)

(P)   9. What was the man on the bed told?
10. There was a lot of talk about what?

(P)   11. What did Bill D. say as Bill W. and Dr.

Bob told their stories?
(5 sentences)

12. When Bill D. said he knew it could not work for him, what did
the two do?

13. What did he have to say about their laughing at him?

(P)   14-a. They then spoke of what?
             14-b. Then what did they tell him?

(P)   16. To which he replied?

(Page 158)

             1-a. He said he prayed and swore
what?
             1-b. How well did it work for him?

(P)   3. What did Bill and Dr. Bob find the next day?

4. What had the prospect been doing?

5. What did he say to them? (2 sentences)

6. Then what did he add?

(P)   7-a. What did the lawyer do on the
third day following his

last drink?

7-b. He further said he was willing to do what?

9-a. How hopeful was his wife when she came to see him?

9-b. What did she think she saw in him?

11. What had begun to take place within him?

If Step Three is taken "honestly and humbly, an effect, sometimes a very great one, is felt at once." p. 63

(P)   12. What happened that afternoon?

13. What did he try to do?

14. How successful was he?

15. But what had he found?

(Page 158 - continued)

(P)   16. When was that?

That was the same month and year Dr. Bob had his last drink.

17. How long was he able to stay sober?

18. What has he regained?

19-a. Who has he helped?
19-b. In what did he become a power?

(P)   21-a. Now, how many sober alcoholics were there?
21-b. What did they believe they must do to survive?

23. Did they find another one right away?

24. How did they find this one?

25-a. What kind of a guy was he?
25-b. What could his parents not determine?

27-a. What kind of people were they?
27-b. They were also shocked by their son's refusal to do what?

(Page 159)
1-a. Was he in pretty bad shape?
1-b. Did he appear to be hopeless?

3-a. What did he consent to do?
3-b. By chance (?), what room did he occupy?

(P) 5. How many visitors did he have?

6. After listening to them for a bit, what did he have to say?
(3 sentences)

7. So now Alcoholics Anonymous had how many members?

(P) 8. All this time, where was Bill W.?

9. How long did he remain in Akron?

10. When he returned to New York, what did he leave?

11. What had these men found?

12-a. What did they know they must do to remain sober?

12-b. That motive became what?

14. Why was that?

15. What did they share with fellow-sufferers?

16. At any time, what were they willing to do?

17. They did what?

18-a. What did they experience?
18-b. Where there were failures, what did they do about the drinker's family?
18-c. This resulted in relieving what?

(P) 21. After eighteen months, how many did they have in the fold?

22-a. Were they close?

22-b. What happened in the evenings?

22-c. What was their constant thought?

25-a. What became customary?

(Page 160)

1-b. Who were these meetings for?

2. Aside from the fellowship and social aspects of the meetings, what were their principal purposes?

(P)   3. Who became interested in what the alcoholics were doing?

4. What did a man and his wife do to support the alcoholics?
The couple was Clarace and T. Henry Williams, non-alcoholic members of the Oxford Group.

5. What did they do with their home?

6. What has many a distracted wife found at the Williams' home?

(P)   7. What have many alcoholic men found

there?

8. What did they come away with?

9. What did he succumb to?
   10-a. With what was he impressed?
   10-b. Where was it that he made that surrender?
   10-c. When did he surrender?

(Page 160 - continued)

13. What appealing characteristics conspired to let the alcoholic know that here was haven at last?

(P)   14. What did the recovered alcoholics and their wives have that made this irresistible?

15. How would the newcomer and his wife feel as they left the Williams' home?

(Page 161)
1. What did they then know?

2. What had they seen?

3. What had they envisioned?

(P)   4. At the time of the writing of this Book,

how many were attending meetings at the Williams' home?

5. Where were the alcoholics coming from?

6. From surrounding towns, what was happening?

7. How many members came from a community (Cleveland) thirty miles away?

8. Since Cleveland was a large place in 1939, what did they anticipate?

(P)   9. Life in A.A. is more than what?

10. What are some of the other activities?

11-a. Who is not welcomed?
11-b. But what is the one requirement?

13. What things are laughed out of countenance?

14. What no longer proved to be of any significance?
(the rest of paragraph)

(P)   15. What started happening in Eastern cities?

16. What was there in one of these cities?
Comment: Townes Hospital

(Page 162)
1. How long ago was it that Bill W. had met Dr. Silkworth?

2. What had many alcoholics experienced at that hospital?
        3-a. To whom are we indebted?
        3-b. Why is that so?

(P)   5. Every few days, what did Dr. Silkworth do?

6. Because he understood our work, what could he do?

7. What did many recovered alcoholics do?
        8-a. What was going on in this Eastern city (New York)?
        8-b. Did many attend?

10. What similarity was there to the Akron Group?

        11-a. What was going on between Akron and New York?
        11-b. What did they foresee?

(P)   13. What is our hope?

14. Was it beginning to happen at the time

this Book was written?

15. What were some of the members?

16-a. What had begun to spring up in other communities?
16-b. Where were they getting their direction?

18. What did members who traveled do?

19. What two good things resulted from this type of activity?

(P)   20. So, they were doing what?

21-a. What can we do?

(Page 163)
1-b. What should you have?
2. What did the authors believe?

(P)   3. What do we know?
4. What are you saying to yourself? (2 sentences)
5. But what?
6. What have you forgotten?
7. What is required to duplicate what the authors accomplished?

(P)   8. Who did they know?

9-a. How long had he lived there?
9-b. What did he find?

11. How long before the writing of this Book was it?

12. Did the authorities care?

Comment: This man was Hank Parkhurst. The alcoholic who authored "Chapter 10, TO EMPLOYERS"

13. What did Hank do?

14. What did the doctor prove to be?

15. Did he check Hank out?

(P)   16. Did Hank talk with the doctor?

17. How well was the doctor impressed?

18. What arrangements were made?

(P)   19. What will our fellow worker soon have?

20-a. What will happen to some of them?

20-b. But if our experience is any criterion, how many will make it?

Comment: Does it appear that we should try to learn how they worked with a new man? If following the clear-cut directions in this Book produced these results, what could we do?

22-a. What will happen when a few men try this Program?

1-b. And will have discovered what as the result of working
with others?

1-c. There will be no stopping until what has happened?

(P)   3. But what may you still say?

4. Can we be sure?

5-a. Who will determine that?
5-b. So Who must you rely on?

7. Who will show you how to have many friends?

(P)   8.   This Book is meant to be what?

9. What do we realize?

10. What will God constantly do?

Comment: *The following is the Twelfth Step Prayer.*

11-a. When should you ask?
11-b. How often should you ask for it?
11-c. What should you ask for?

14. What is the promise?

15. But you obviously cannot do what?

16-a. So, what must we see to?
16-b. What is the promise of this?

18. What is this for us?

(P)   19. We should abandon ourselves to Whom?
Comment: Steps Three, Six & Seven?
(Page 164 - continued)

20. Admit our faults to whom?
Comment: Steps Four and Five?

21. We are to clear away what?
Comment: Steps Eight and Nine?

22. We should then do what?
Comment: Step Twelve?

23-a. How shall we be with you?
23-b. Where will we meet?

MAIN POINTS

1. Suicide is a danger to the suffering alcoholic when

emotional issues overwhelm him or her.

2. This chapter brings hope to recovering alcoholics.

3. This chapter demonstrates that a "spiritual experience" and a life lived on spiritual principles is necessary for sustained recovery.

4. This chapter helps us see that continued spiritual action in the Twelve Steps helps us take a daily inventory to stay in God's will and also be guided in situations that used to baffle us.

CHAPTER 14

DOCTOR BOB'S NIGHTMARE (171-181)

(P)   1. Where was Dr. Bob born?

2. In his youth, what was far above average?

3. Were beer and liquor readily available?

4. Could anybody buy alcoholic beverages?

5. How were the men who had booze imported looked upon?

6. What facilities were plentiful in his town?

(P)   7. How did he describe his parents?

(Page 172)

1. What about his parents' I.Q.?

(P)   2-a. What did he consider to be an unfortunate situation?
2-b. What did he suspect it produced?

(P)   4. In his early years, what was he forced to do?

5. What effect did this have on him?

6. Was he a man of his word?

(P)   7. What came after high school?

8. Was he in the minority?

9. How was his drinking?

10. What was he able to do that was better than most?

11-a. What did he never have?
11-b. Therefore, he believed what?

13-a. What was his life centered around?
13-b. Without regard to what?

15. With what distinction did he graduate?

(P)   16. Where was he and what did he do for the next

three years?

(Page 173)

1. What else did he do during these years?

2. How many days work did he lose during those three years due to drinking?

(P)   3. What was the next thing he did?

4. Besides studying medicine, what else did he do?

5-a. To what was he elected?
5-b. Did he do well in that social group?

7. What did he experience on many mornings?
8-a. How did his sophomore year go?
8-b. Since he found himself in trouble, what did he do?

10-a. After he dried out, what did he think?

10-b. What did he do?

12. Did he have trouble getting back into school?

13. What was he able to do?

14. Was the faculty excited to have him back?

15. What was he forced to do?

(Page 174)

(P)   1-a. Had his drinking progressed?
1-b. Who went to a lot of trouble to try to

help him?

     3. How successful were his father's efforts?

(P)   4. With final exams coming up, what did he do?

     5. What problem did he experience as the result of his spree?

     6. What did he turn in for his tests?

       7-a. As the result, what was he forced to do?

       7-b. What requirement was placed on him?

     9. Was he successful?

(P)   10. As the result of staying dry and giving school his best shot, what did he receive?

     11. How did those two years go?

(P)   12. At the end of the two years, what did Dr. Bob do?

     13. What was it he had at that time?

       14-a. What did he soon discover?
       14-b. So, what happened then?

(P)   16-a. Was he still enjoying his drinking?
       16-b. Seeking relief, what did he do?

(Page 175)
1. Why did Dr. Bob say that?

2-a. At the end of three years, what happened?

2-b. What did he persuade his friends to do?

2-c. Or he resorted to what?

(P)   5-a. At this point, what did his father do?
5-b. How long was he confined?

7. At the end of two months, what did he do?

8. This episode scared him sufficiently to cause him to do what?

(P)   9. What Constitutional Amendment gave him a sense of security?
10. Why did he believe that?

11. Consequently, it would make no great difference even if he what?

12. What two things was he unaware of?

13-a. So how did he start drinking?
13-b. What happened in a short time?

(P)   15. Over the next two years what happened?

16. What were they?

17-a. Since he was not blessed with an abundance of money, what was he forced to do?

(Page 176)

1-b. The result of this would be what?

2. Most of the time, how did Dr. Bob handle his need?

3. But occasionally he would do what?

4-a. This was not good because it lessened his chances to do what?
4-b. Which in turn would mean what?

6-a. Over the next fifteen years, what did he not do?
6-b. And seldom did what?

8-a. Where would he hide during the day?
8-b. On occasions, he would do what?

10. What usually happened?

(P)   11. What would he do when his wife, Anne, would plan to be away?

12. What else did he make use of?

13-a. What did he never use?
13-b. Why?

15. Why was he lucky there?

16. What else did he hide small bottles in?

17. What would his bootlegger do for him?

18. Sometimes he would mess up and bring it home how?

(Page 177)
1. What else did he used to do?

2. When did that great idea quit working?

(P)   3. What will we not learn of?

(P)   4. By this time, who abandoned us?
            5-a. Why were invitations not being
extended to the Smith family?
            5-b. What did Anne dare not do?

            7-a. His fear of sleeplessness demanded
what of him?
            7-b. But to be sure that he had what he
needed, what did he find he had to do?
        9. How long did this routine continue?

        10. What was his nightmare?
            11-a. What promise did he make?

            11-b. How successful was he with his
promises?

(P)   13. For the experimentally inclined, what
experiment does he
            refer to?

        14. What made him feel safe?

        15. What could he do with that stuff?

        16. Why did he say it was harmless?

        17. Who said he could fill the place with beer?

        18. Before long, what was he doing?

        19. What did this do for him?
                (Page 178)
            1-a. Then what occurred to him?
            1-b. So what did he begin to do then?
        3. What were the results?

(P)   4. About the same time, he joined up with what
kind of people?

5. What were they able to do that Dr. Bob couldn't do?

6. More important, they seemed to be what?

7. How did Dr. Bob describe himself at this time?

8. What did he sense?

9-a. What kind of thing was it they had?
9-b. How did that strike him?
9-c. But how did he feel about it?

12-a. How long had he been trying the Oxford Program?
12-b. What were the results?

14. What else did he do?

(P)   15-a. What did Anne do?
15-b. How did that affect him?
15-c. What was he unable to sense?

18. What was Anne able to do that Dr. Bob could not understand?

19. Had Anne not kept her faith, what did Dr. Bob know would have happened to him?

20. What gift have alcoholics been given?

21. What can we never explain?

(Page 179)
(P)   1. After two and one half years with the Oxford Group, what happened one Saturday afternoon?
2-a. It was May 11, 1935 the day before what day of celebration?
2-b. What had Dr. Bob brought home to

commemorate that day?

        2-c. What condition was he in and what did he do about it?

    5. What happened the next day?

        6-a. Wishing to be polite, what did he agree to do?

        6-b. For how long was he willing to do it?

(P)   8-a. When did he and Anne arrive at the Gate House of the Seiberling Estate?

        8-b. How long did the fifteen minutes last?

        10-a. What did he later have with Bill?

        10-b. What happened as an apparent result of their talks?

        12-a. How long did it last?

        12-b. Where did Dr. Bob go?

        14-a. What did he relieve the train of?

        14-b. Then he purchased what?

    16. What day was that?

        17-a. What did he do that night?

        17-b. What did he do on Monday?

        17-c. And then he proceeded to do what?

    20. Where did he do his drinking?

    21. How did Tuesday go?

(Page 179 - continued)

    22. To avoid embarrassment, what did he do?

    23. Where did he head for and what did he get on

the way?

24. What did he have to wait for?

25-a. What did he experience at that
point?

25-b. Where did he come to?

27-a. What did they do?
27-b. What did Anne do?

29-a. What did Bill do with Dr. Bob?

(Page 180)
1-b. What did Bill give Dr. Bob that
night?

1-c. What did he give him the next
morning?

(P)   3. What day was that?
4. How long had Dr. Bob been sober when he
wrote his story?

(P)   5. What question would naturally come to the
mind of most people?

6. What must be remembered?

7-a. What had Bill experienced that made
the difference for Dr. Bob?
7-b. What had each of these two men
tried that worked for Bill but did not work for Dr. Bob?

9. What information did Bill have that Dr. Bob
did not have?

10-a. What was the single most important
thing that helped Dr. Bob?

10-b. In other words, Bill did what?

12. What did Bill know?

(P)   13. What was a most wonderful blessing?

14. What three things did he say he had regained?

15. What other two things were good?

(P)   16. What did Dr. Bob say he did with great deal of his time?

17. Does he tell us why?

(Page 181)

1. Reason one?

2. Reason two?

3. Reason three?

4. Reason four?

(P)   5-a. What did Dr. Bob experience in early sobriety?

5-b. How long did this last?

7. Was it an occasional thing?

8. But at no time was he what?

9-a. What used to upset him?

9-b. What thinking did he develop to combat this?

11-a. It didn't behoove him to what?

11-b. Why was that?

(P)   13-a. What kind of folks did he mention?

13-b. That would keep them from what?

13-c. What were his feelings for those folks?

16. What if you think you can handle your drinking on you own?
17-a. But if you really and truly want to do what?
17-b. And sincerely feel you need what?
17-c. What do we know?

20-a. Is it a reliable way?
20-b. If you will do what?

CHAPTER 15

SECOND STUDY GUIDE

About This Study Guide

This material was found in 2004 via Internet by an AA member in Sweden who then used it in a group with other AA members. The group experience was positive and can be recommended for anyone considering it as a help in working AA's Twelve Steps.

This material was made and used during the early 1990's by North American members of AA who chose to remain anonymous. It is therefore not possible to prove authorship. Users are welcome to spread this material as they wish.

The original material was designed to be used in groups. If however you wish to use this material solely together with your sponsor that works, too. Just ignore the references for use in larger groups of 8-12 people.

This study material sticks closely to AA's Big Book of Alcoholics Anonymous. There are many page references to help each person working the steps to easily refer back to AA's major text.

It may be helpful to point out what is at times a source of confusion for AA members: that AA's first three steps cannot be found in numerical order in the Big Book. However, any person studying the first five and a half chapters of Alcoholics Anonymous can be assured of covering all three of AA's first three steps.

It may also be helpful to point out that this study material is more detailed in the first four steps than in the remaining ones.

STEP STUDY TEAMS 1. Purpose

1. (a) To provide the person who has not worked the Steps with motivation and assistance in working the Steps.
2. (b) To provide those who have worked the Steps with an opportunity and motivation to do it again and to share your experience.

2. Plan

1. (a) Teams of no more than 12 persons will be formed (8 to 10 are preferred). The make-up of each team will be approximately 3 to 4 members who have worked the Steps in the manner described in the Big Book and 8 to 9 members

who have never worked the Steps in this manner, but who are willing to try.

2. (b) Each team will select its own meeting place and meeting time, preferably at a time which does not conflict with the 8:00 p.m. meetings of A.A. (Team meetings are not a substitute for A.A. Group activity and fellowship.)

3. (c) At the initial meeting all present will:

(1) Exchange telephone numbers and addresses and select a meeting place.

(2) (3)

(4) (5)

(6)

Commit to stay with the team until all members have completed the Steps.

Commit to do the Steps according to the Big Book as augmented by the 12 Steps and 12 Traditions (including on the knees 3rd Step with others -- a 4th and 5th Step and all the rest).

Those persons who have not done the Steps will be asked to commit to do them at least once more with another team.

Commit to making telephone or personal contact with one or more members of the team during each week the Steps are being taken and sharing your problem or experience with the assignment that week.

Commit to attend the meetings except on rare and extremely unusual circumstances. Each member really needs to be present each week. If a member cannot be present, another member should be called and advised of the problem so that the team will not delay the meetings.

After the initial meeting, no one will be added to the team. If someone has a slip or is not living up to their commitment to the team, the other members of the team must decide if they want to allow them to continue with the team.

(e) When the team has completed the Steps, it will disband. The estimated time to complete the Steps is 15 - 20 weeks.

(d)

3. **Meeting Format**

(a) There is no formal meeting format and each group is free to select its own. Most groups rotate the chairmanship from week to week and simply discuss the assigned material and share their experiences in applying it to their life.

(b) Each member must come to the meeting having read and studied those portions of the Big Book and 12 x 12 which relate to the Step under consideration and having done his or her assignment.

(c) The function of the team will be to apply the principals of each Step to their lives and share their experience in a discussion of each Step.

(d) It is suggested that each member of the team obtain a study notebook to record his or her notes, assignments, 4th Step, etc.

(e) A 4th Step will be written and a substantial period of time (all that is needed) will be spent in analysis of this Step and resolving any problems that arise. If any group member encounters any problem that requires additional assistance, it will be available.

4. As teams complete the Steps, new teams will be formed to help newcomers and others who want to participate. A nucleus of experienced member (3-4) should accept new members on a first-come first-served basis.

5. It is suggested that the teams not be co-ed because of the 4th Step problems.

6. Caution: The step team should become a very sharing group. When there is deep sharing, the meetings can last so long as to be an inconvenience or burden to some members. Since we are trying to learn to be considerate, it is suggested that the meeting proper be limited to approximately one hour and that each speaker limit his/her remarks to his/her part of that hour. Longer and more difficult problems can then be shared with those who have more time. Also, call each other throughout the week - you don't need to wait for meetings to share.

STEP STUDY OUTLINE AND ASSIGNMENT SHEET

The following is a suggested assignment sheet and outline for use by the Step Study Team. The time given for any particular study can be extended or shortened as each team chooses. It is suggested that, before the study is completed, each team member will have read the entire text of the book

Alcoholics Anonymous.

Week No. 1:

Meet and follow the outline regarding the Purpose, Plan and Meeting Format of the Step Study Teams. It is important that the commitment section of this outline be carefully reviewed and that each member of the team thoroughly understands that he or she is committing to do the Steps -- all of the Steps. It should be understood that everyone will probably have one or more absences, and perfect attendance is not absolutely required. It is most helpful that everyone be present as much as possible and that communication develop between the team members so that they know how the other team members are progressing and how they are feeling about the team study.

At the initial meeting the team members should have read the Preface, Foreword of the First Edition, Second Edition and Third Edition. Note the Foreword to the Third Edition states: To show other alcoholics precisely how we have recovered is the main purpose of this book. Compare this language with the language on Page 29 at the end of Chapter Two where it is stated: Further on, clear cut directions are given showing how we recover. This is the task this team is about to undertake.

Read and discuss the doctor's opinion at the meeting. These and other questions will occur to the group, and each should be discussed in some depth.

1. Were you aware that your illness affected both your mind and your body?
2. Do you believe or can you accept the concept of an allergic reaction to alcohol?
3. What is an allergy?
4. Do you agree with the concept of hospitalization?
5. Have you ever experienced the phenomena of craving (page xxvi)?
6. Did you like the effect of alcohol?
7. Did you reach the point where you could not differentiate the true from the false?

8. Did your alcoholic life seem normal?
9. The doctor seems to say that a psychic change must occur -- what is a psychic change?
10. Can you accept the fact that alcoholism has never been, by any treatment with which we are familiar, permanently eradicated?

ASSIGNMENT:

Buy your workbook and begin to note your own reaction
to the matters set forth in the doctor's opinion. In
summary, begin to write how was I powerless over
alcohol. It is equally important to write any reservation
you may have that you are, in fact, powerless over
alcohol.

Read Chapter One, "Bill's Story", and be prepared to
discuss this matter as it applies to your life in the
second week.

Week No. 2:

Chapter One, "Bill's Story".

1. Did you ever ask, "Was I crazy?" (Page 5)
2. Did you ever feel the remorse, horror and
   hopelessness of the next morning?

   (Page 6)

3. Did your mind ever race uncontrollably? (Page 6)
4. Did you ever seek oblivion? (Page 6)
5. Did you feel lonely? (Page 8)
6. Did you feel fear? (Page 8)
7. What was your reaction to religion, the church
   and God? (Page 10)

Note what happened to Bill's prejudice against their
God when he began to apply his own concept of God
(Page 12).

8. Did you know that "nothing more was required
   of me to make my beginning" than willingness or
   a willingness to believe?
9. Doesn't Bill essentially take the first through the
   eleventh Step at this time? (Page 13) Notice how
   Bill was instructed to find God's will and pray
   (Page 13).

10. Has your common sense become "uncommon sense" in this manner? (Page 13)
11. Bill really takes the twelfth Step on Page 14, doesn't he? The program worked in all of Bill's affairs -- Page 15.

The foregoing are simply samples of questions that may occur or points that may be raised.

12. What was of particular significance to you in this chapter?
13. What did you find that you could not agree with or which you could not accept?

ASSIGNMENT:

Read Chapter Two and be prepared to discuss how you react to this chapter next week. Continue to write how you are powerless over alcohol and begin to consider what you can truly manage in your life. As thoughts occur to you about whether you can or cannot manage life and in particular your life, write down your thoughts in your notebook.

Week No. 3:

Chapter Two, "There Is a Solution". Again, having read this chapter:

1. What parts of the chapter can you apply to your life?
2. What is your reaction to the membership of Alcoholics Anonymous?
3. Did your alcoholism "engulf all whose lives touched the sufferer's" (Page 18)?
4. What was their reaction?
5. Do you see how you can reach another alcoholic (Page 18)? Note on Page 20 the book answers the question, "What do I have to do?"
6. Have you been asked the questions on Page 20 by yourself or other people?

7. What were the answers?
8. From your examination of yourself in the past weeks and your reading of this chapter, are you a "real alcoholic"? (Page 21)
9. If not, why not? Discuss this with your team.
10. Did you have control over alcohol, did you do absurd and incredible and tragic things while drinking, were you a Jekyll and Hyde?

These questions and observations on Page 21 may help you in answering the questions you have been writing about, having to do with your powerlessness over alcohol.

11. Why did we drink the way we did? (Page 22)
12. Why do we take that one drink?
13. What has become of the common sense and the will power that he/she still sometimes displays with respect to other matters?
14. Did you ask yourself these questions?
15. Had you lost the power of choice described on Page 24?
16. Have you ever said, "What's the use anyhow" (or something similar)?

There is a solution (Page 25). The great fact is just this and nothing less. That we have had deep and effective spiritual experiences. Read and understand Appendix II and the rest of this paragraph because it is an outstanding summary of what happens in the program.

Our alternative to the solution is to "go on blotting out the consciousness of our intolerable situation as best we could or to accept spiritual help." (Page 25)

Note that Appendix II is referred to again on Page 27.
ASSIGNMENT:
Read Chapter Three and discuss how it applies to your life for the next week. **Week No. 4:**
Chapter Three, "More About Alcoholism".

1. Did you have the "great obsession" (Page 30)?
2. Did you know that was an illusion?

3. Did you try to control your drinking, and can you diagnose yourself? (Page 31)
4. Has your writing in your book listed those things you attempted to do to control your use of alcohol and your failures?
5. Do you have a reservation of any kind or any lurking notion that you will some day be immune to alcohol? (Page 33)
6. Can you identify with the mental status that precede a relapse into drinking, and do you understand that these mental states are the crux of the problem? (Page 35)
7. Do you understand why an actual or potential alcoholic will be absolutely unable to stop drinking on the basis of self-knowledge? (Page 39)

Note the doctor's reaction to alcoholism on Page 43. Also note the solution at the bottom of Page 43.

ASSIGNMENT:

Read and be prepared to discuss Chapter Four next week. By now you should have completed writing most of your memories about why you are powerless over alcohol and why your life is unmanageable. If you are having difficulty with these problems, discuss this with the team members or your sponsor.

Week No. 5:

Chapter Four, "We Agnostics".

1. Do you accept the fact that you have only two alternatives if you are an alcoholic - an alcoholic death or to live a life on a spiritual basis? (Page 44)

2. Have you lacked power to manage life (Page 45)? Note that the "main object of this book is to enable you to find a Power greater than yourself which will solve your problem."
3. Have you had honest doubts and prejudices about God? (Page 45)
4. What has been your reaction to the word "God" -- what will He look like, what will it be like when you find Him, and where did you get these ideas?
5. Had you abandoned the idea of God entirely? (Page 45)
6. Are you willing to lay aside your previous beliefs or prejudice and express even a willingness to believe in a Power greater than yourself?
7. What is your concept of God? (Page 46)
8. Do you now believe or are you even willing to believe that there is a Power greater than yourself? (Page 47)
9. Do you recognize that when you can say "yes" to this question that you are "on your way"? (Page 47)
10. Note that the book once again refers you to Appendix II at this point. What is it that Appendix II says that is indispensable?
11. Have you been open-minded or have you been obstinate, sensitive and unreasonably prejudiced about discussion about God? (Page 48)
12. What reservations do you have when you have read this chapter?
13. Have you been biased and unreasonably prejudiced about the realm of the spirit? (Page 51)

14. Did your ideas work -- will the God idea work? (Page 52)
15. ARE YOU REALLY READY TO FEARLESSLY FACE AND ANSWER THE

PROPOSITION THAT "EITHER GOD IS EVERYTHING OR HE IS NOTHING.

GOD EITHER IS, OR HE ISN'T. WHAT IS YOU CHOICE TO BE?" (Page 53)

16. Do you believe that "when we drew near to Him, He disclosed himself to us!"?

(Page 57)

17. Remember what it said on Page 28? If what we have learned and felt and seen means anything at all, it means that all of us, whatever our race, creed, or colour are children of a living Creator with whom we may form a relationship upon simple and understandable terms as soon as we are willing and honest enough to try.

ASSIGNMENT:

In your notebook, write what you can believe about a Power greater than yourself. On another page write what you cannot believe about God. As you go forward from this point, it is those things which you believe or which fit into your conception of God which you will be using and you can be comforted in knowing that our own conception, however inadequate, was "sufficient to make the approach and to effect a contact with Him." (Page 46) Read and be prepared to discuss Chapter Five in the book next week.

Week No. 6:

Chapter Five, "How It Works". Discuss the materials contained in this chapter from Page 58 to Page 63 (i.e., through the part which concludes Step 3).

1. Do you question whether you are capable of being honest with yourself? (If you do – you're not.) Note the state of mind you're asked to have when you start the Steps -- Honesty, fearlessness, thoroughness, and a willingness to go to any length.

2. What do half measures avail us?
3. Are you convinced that a life run on self-will can hardly be a success? (Page 60)
4. Can you see the effects of self-centeredness in your life?
5. How have you been self-centered? List examples in your workbook and discuss them with the group.
6. Did you know that you could not reduce self-centeredness much by wishing or

   trying on your own power? (Page 62)

7. Are you willing to make the decisions set forth at the bottom of Page 62?
8. Note the promises that follow the taking of Step 3 as described at the top of Page

   63. Are you willing to take this Step?

Many groups at this point commit one to the other that they are going to take this Step and recite the prayer that is set forth on Page 63 together.

ASSIGNMENT:

Continue to list places where you can see that you are self-centered in your workbook and commence the fourth Step using the Step 4 Guide (coming up soon). To accomplish this, take the action suggested in the Instructions 1 and 2 of the Guide, including the preparation of a Grudge List.

Week No. 7:

Discuss Instruction I and your Grudge List.

STEP 4 GUIDE

Many readers find the instructions for Step 4 contained in the book Alcoholics Anonymous confusing and complex. This paper is written to reflect the experience of certain members of the fellowship of Alcoholics Anonymous in analyzing these instructions and their experience in taking this step in accordance with the instructions given in this book. Those who have taken this step in the manner suggested in the Big Book, including the inventory, the analysis, and the study and prayer suggested by the Book have found it to be an exciting and rewarding experience. This experience is available to anyone who will complete each of the following steps to the best of his/her ability in the order in which they are given. Perfection is not required, but a good effort involving honesty, open-mindedness and willingness is essential. Do not skip any instruction and complete each instruction before proceeding to the next.

INSTRUCTION 1:
Read the following and understand what we are doing.

I. The Time and Purposes of Step Four

Perhaps the greatest promise by the program of Alcoholics Anonymous is that God, as you understand Him, will do for you what you cannot do for yourself. This promise carries with it the obvious condition that you must do what you can.

When you have made the decision required by Step 3, the Big Book warns us "although our decision was a vital and crucial step, it could have little permanent effect unless at once followed by a strenuous effort to face, and be rid of, the things in ourselves which have been blocking us (from God) ... so we had to get down to causes and conditions. Therefore, we started upon a personal inventory."

The specific instructions for taking this step are contained from Page 64 to Page 71 of the book Alcoholics Anonymous. These instructions should be read carefully at this point.

II. What Do We Seek?

The inventory is described as a "fact-finding and fact-facing process." We are said to be seeking the truth about ourselves and to honestly take stock of our lives. We are to search out the flaws in our makeup which caused our failure. Throughout the book

Alcoholics Anonymous it is stated that self, selfishness and self-centeredness were the root of our troubles. Being convinced that self, manifested in various ways, was what had defeated us, we considered its common manifestations. These common manifestations are grouped in three categories -- resentment, fear and sex relationships. Each of these common manifestations is treated separately in the inventory.

III. Resentments -- The Number One Offender

From these thoughts or mental attitudes stem "all forms of spiritual disease." We are instructed to list all people, institutions or principles with whom we were angry or had resentments. What is a resentment?

1. (a) Webster's Dictionary defines resentment as "indignation or ill-will felt as a result of a real or imagined offense." Webster's then refers the reader to the word "anger" and gives other examples of this thought or feeling, which include rage, fury, ire, wrath, resentment and indignation. These words denote varying degrees of displeasure, from anger - strong, intense and explosive - to the longer lasting resentment - ill-will and suppressed anger generated by a sense of being wronged or being wrong.

2. (b) In summary and broadly defined, we are dealing with a negative or unpleasant thought or feeling caused or generated by the real or imagined act or failure to act of a person, institution, or principle.

3. (c) Persons, institutions or principles may need some explanation. Remember you are a person and your action or failure to act may very well cause you to think or feel bad (generally, this resentment of ourselves is call guilt). Institutions are any group of people, authorities, companies, governmental agencies, or other organizations.

A principle is a basic truth or law. Many of these basic truths or laws have and do offend us, for example:

1. Alcoholism is an incurable, progressive disease.
2. Honesty is the best policy.
3. As you give, you receive -- (each of us suffers the consequences of his own action -- there is no free lunch).
4. When you are disturbed, no matter what the cause, there is something wrong with you.
5. A life lived without self-examination is not worth living. (Socrates)

Preparing the Grudge List

With the foregoing instructions in mind, a list should be prepared of the people, institutions or principles which have or do cause you to have a resentment, as defined above.

Certain points should be remembered.
1. If you can remember the resentment, you should list it, even though you think you are over it. Go back through your life - nothing counts but thoroughness and honesty.

2. A review of family albums, school annuals and the like may help you be thorough. Some people write a short autobiography of their life to assist them in their memory.
3. Do not concern yourself with whether you should or should not have the feeling -- just make the list and nothing more at this point.

4. Throughout the taking of Step 4 and at times thereafter, you will recall other people, institutions and principles which have caused these negative thoughts and feelings. You can add to this list at any time, but do not spend too much time worrying about how complete the list is. Simply do the best you can over a reasonable period of time (perhaps a week).

INSTRUCTION 2:

Make a list of the people institutions and principles you resent.

INSTRUCTION 3:

When you have completed your Grudge List, and not before, purchase and mark a spiral notebook as described below. At this time we will begin to analyze our resentments.

(a) Analysis of Resentments. When you have completed your list and not before, each resentment must be analyzed. Step 4 will mean very little unless you come to understand each resentment and learn from it. The following procedure has proven helpful in this understanding and analysis:

1. Purchase a spiral notebook and open it so that you have a blank page on either side of the wire spiral. With a ruler or straight-edge, divide each of these pages vertically so that when both pages are divided, you have a total of four columns. Turn the page and repeat this process until you have divided several pages in this manner. The drawing below may help you understand this instruction.
2. The columns on each page should be labeled as follows:

Column 1:
Column 2:
Column 3:
Column 4 should be left blank for the time being.

Name Cause Affect

NAME	CAUSE	AFFECT	

INSTRUCTION 4:

One at a time you must take each resentment from your Grudge List and enter it into Column 1, then complete 2 and 3 as described below. Complete the analysis of each resentment before taking the next one from the Grudge List. The following is a step by step description of this instruction:

(a) Take the first name from your Grudge List and write it in Column 1 on the first page.

(b) In Column 2, write a few words which describe each and every event or circumstance you can recall which causes you to resent the person named in Column 1. This is a very important part of the analysis -- we learn from specific events, not general complaints (for example, we learn little from the complaint that "he was always lying" but we learn much from a specific "he told me he wasn't married.")

(c) Opposite each of the events you have listed in Column 2, write the reason the event or circumstance bothered you. Specifically, ask yourself;

1. (1) Did it affect my self-esteem (the way I think of myself or want others to think of me)?

2. (2) Did it affect my pocketbook?
3. (3) Did it affect my ambition (what I wanted or needed)?
4. (4) Was one of my personal relationships affected or threatened?
5. (5) If the effects described in questions 1 through 4 above do not accurately describe the effect the event had upon you, write a few words to explain how you felt and how you were affected.
6. (6) COMPLETE THE ANALYSIS OF EACH OF YOUR RESENTMENTS

   ARISING OUT OF EACH OF THE EVENTS BEFORE GOING FURTHER WITH THE INVENTORY.

INSTRUCTION 5:

When Columns 1-3 have been completed for each resentment, take a little time to look back over them and then take the following action.

(a) Study and Prayer. Read and study the Big Book from the paragraph that begins at the bottom of Page 65 through the second paragraph on Page 67. Ask yourself these questions about each resentment and each event causing it and write a brief paragraph reflecting your answers.

1. (1) Having determined who was at fault, did I go further in my study of this event?
2. (2) Did I try to retaliate, fight back or run? What was the result? Did it help?
3. (3) Is it clear to you that a life which includes one of these resentments leads only to futility and unhappiness? Has the resentment ever benefited you in any way, or have you squandered hours thinking about the resentment? Do you realize and understand that these thoughts "separate you from the sunlight of

the Spirit" (God)? Do you know that these thoughts will lead you to the insanity of the first drink, and with us, to drink is to die?

4. (4) Do you understand that through our thoughts and reactions to people, places and things, the world and its people dominate us? Do you understand that until we progress beyond the point of simply stop blaming ourselves and others, there can be no growth or solution?

5. (5) Can you forgive?

6. (6) Do you recognize that other people have the same problem with life that

you have had and many of them are spiritually sick?

7. (7) Honestly pray the 4th Step prayer -- God, help me show

_____, the same tolerance, pity and patience that I would cheerfully grant a sick friend.

_____ is a sick person, how can I be helpful to him/her? Save me from being angry. Thy will be done. From this point forward we try to avoid retaliation or argument.

Beginning of Growth. As noted earlier, it is a spiritual axiom that when I am disturbed, no matter what the cause, there is something the matter with me. Now that you have listed and understood the resentment and how it affected you, having stopped blaming or putting out of your mind the wrongs others have done, you can now look for your own actions or reactions. In the past we went no further than to declare that someone was wrong. Isn't it true that we acted or reacted during each event or circumstance? Didn't we become angry? Depressed? Filled with self-pity, envy, jealously, etc.? Didn't this affect our lives and the lives of those close to us?

INSTRUCTION 6:

Complete Column 4 as follows:

1. At the top of the fourth column on each page, insert the words "my faults or mistakes."
2. For each person, institution or principle and for each event, ask yourself:

(b) The

1. Where have I been selfish, dishonest, self-seeking, and frightened?
2. Where was I to blame?
3. How did I act or react? How did this affect me and those close to me?

3. Write down your faults as revealed by the above questions in the fourth column opposite each person, institution or principle and each event.

When you have concluded all of the instructions with respect to resentments, and not before, proceed to "fear".

INSTRUCTION 7:

List your fears.

IV. Fear -- Touches every aspect of our lives.

Read from the third paragraph appearing on Page 67 of the Big Book through the first three paragraphs on Page 68. Then take the following action:

1. (a) "Fear" defined. Webster's Dictionary defines "fear" as a feeling of alarm or disquiet caused by the expectation of danger, pain, disaster or the like (being found out, being known for what you know or think you are). It is said that the driving force in the life of most alcoholics is the self-

centered fear that we will lose something we have or that we will not get something we think we need or want.

2. (b) Listing of Fears. On a page following the section on resentments, write a short description of each fear that you have experienced. Remember, under the topic "Resentments" (2a, above) you have already asked yourself about the impact of fear on your resentments. We now complete the list of times, places and circumstances which evoke this feeling (i.e., snakes, bugs, heights, women, men, etc.).

INSTRUCTION 8:

Write a short analysis of each fear.

(c)

Analysis of Fear. Having listed each of the fears, we should write a short analysis of these fears in our effort to understand them. It is said that each of these fears sets in motion chains of circumstances which brought about or caused us misfortunes. Can you cite examples where this occurred? Why do you have each fear? Was it because self-reliance failed? Were you about to be harmed in some way by something you could not control or avoid? Can you run away from fear? How did I act or react to fear? Did my fear affect others? What should we now rely upon, if not ourselves?

INSTRUCTION 9:

Read and understand the solution to fear.
(a) Study and Prayer. When our fears have been listed and the above questions answered, the book Alcoholics Anonymous gives us the solution to fear in the second and third paragraphs appearing on Page 68. We are also given a short prayer in which we ask Him to remove our fears and direct our attention to what He would have us

to be. This solution and prayer should be directed toward each of your fears.

V. Sex-Relationships

This section of the inventory is covered in the book Alcoholics Anonymous from the last paragraph commencing on Page 68 through the end of Chapter 5. This material should be read at this point.

(a) Scope of Inventory. This portion of the inventory begins by clearly discussing sexual relationships. However, in the last sentence of the last paragraph ending on Page 70, it states "we have listed the people we have hurt by our conduct and are willing to straighten out the past if we can." This sentence indicates a broader view of our relationships is important, and it is therefore suggested that we review our relationship with each of the important people in our lives, as well as all sexual relationships.

INSTRUCTION 10:

List those persons who are important in your life and any other person affected by your drinking or self-centeredness.

(b) Preparing a List of Relationships. Following "fears" in your inventory book, you should list the names of the persons to be studies. These should include both sexual and other relationships, including family, business, friends, etc.

INSTRUCTION 11:

Write a brief paragraph about each relationship.

(c) With respect to each person named on your list of relationships, write a short paragraph which answers the following questions -- remember to deal with specific events.

1. Was I selfish in this relationship?
2. Was I dishonest in this relationship?
3. Was I considerate in this relationship?
4. Whom did I hurt?
5. Did I arouse jealousy?
6. Did I arouse suspicion?
7. Did I arouse bitterness?
8. Was I at fault?
9. What should I have done?

(d) Study and Prayer. Through study and prayer, we seek to shape sane and sound ideals for our future sex life and our relationships. Whatever our ideals turn out to be, we must be willing to grow toward them. We must be willing to make amends for past wrongs, providing we do not bring about still more harm in so doing. In prayer and meditation we ask God what we should do about each specific matter, and we are told the right answer will come if we want it.

On Page 70 in the first paragraph, we are given instructions on how to proceed toward our new ideal.

In summary we are told to pray for the right ideal, for guidance in each questionable situation, for sanity, and for strength to do the right thing. In these troublesome areas we are told to throw ourselves into helping others.

VI. Summary

Read the last two paragraphs of Chapter 5. It is also helpful to read chapter 4 of the Twelve Steps and Twelve Traditions at this point. Have you left anything out of your inventory? Have you failed to list any event or subject the memory of which causes you to be uncomfortable? If so, you should write it down now.

CONGRATULATIONS, YOU HAVE COMPLETED STEP FOUR

VII. STEP FIVE

Read Pages 72 though the first full paragraph on Page 75 -- take Step 5.

ASSIGNMENT:

Next week you should take the action described in Instructions 3-5 of the guide.

Week No. 8.

Discuss the findings you have made on Instructions 1-5 of the Guide and any problems you are having.

ASSIGNMENT:

Follow Instruction 6 and complete any work you have not completed on Instructions 1 through 6 for the next week.

Week No. 9:

Discuss the work you have done in Instruction 1 through 6 of the inventory process and any problems that you are having. The group should assist anyone in taking the inventory that is having difficulty and this may include spending some time with them during the week.

ASSIGNMENT:
Follow Instructions 7, 8 and 9 of the Guide. **Week No. 10:**

Review your writing required in Instructions 7, 8 and 9 and discuss any problems that you or any other member of the group is having.

ASSIGNMENT:

Assignment for the next week is to complete Instructions 10 and 11 of the inventory process.

Week No. 11:

Review and discuss your writing on sex in generalities -- no specifics and no war stories are needed, lest matters of pride and self-centeredness become involved in the meeting.

ASSIGNMENT:

Your assignment for the next week is to find someone to take a 5th Step with and make a specific date for this 5th Step. Also read Chapter Six and be prepared to discuss this chapter.

Week No. 12:

Chapter Six "Into Action". Discuss Page 72 through Page 75. Has everyone had a good experience with this Step? Are there reservations about doing the 5th Step and, if so, what are they? Have you skimped on the program to this point? Take your 5th Step.

ASSIGNMENT:
Read Chapters Six and Seven, in Twelve Steps and Twelve Traditions.

Week No. 13:

Chapters Six and Seven, in Twelve Steps and Twelve Traditions. Discuss these chapters along the lines you have previously discussed the earlier chapters in the book, Alcoholics Anonymous. Particularly, you should attempt to itemize and list those defects of character which you have which you recognize stand in the way of your usefulness to your fellows. Which defects of character do you have which do not stand in the way of your usefulness to your fellows? Discuss willingness and humility and what they mean in context with these Steps.

ASSIGNMENT:

Next week be prepared to discuss the material on Page 76 through 84 and read the eighth and ninth chapters in Twelve Steps and Twelve Traditions.

Week No. 14:

Discuss the material you have read.

1. Do you have misgiving about these Steps? (Page 76)
2. Do you feel diffident about going to some of these people?
3. What is your real purpose (Page 77)?
4. Is timing important in this Step?
5. Can you approach the people on your eight Step list in a helpful and forgiving spirit?

(Page 77) (see Pages 66-67)

6. Do you recognize that nothing worthwhile can be accomplished until you clean your side of the street? (Page 78)
7. Is it important that you be praised for your ninth Step efforts? (Page 78)
8. Have you discussed any criminal offenses you may have committed and which may still be open with your sponsor? If not, you certainly should do so. (See Page 79)
9. Do you understand how your ninth Step may harm other people? (See Page 79)
10. Have you studied your domestic troubles and the harm that may have been caused in these areas?
11. Do you understand the importance of not creating further harm by creating further jealousy and resentment in a tell-all session? (Page 81)
12. What does the author mean when he says that the spiritual life is not a theory -- we have to live it? (Page 83)
13. Do you see that in making the ninth Step you should be sensible, tactful, considerate and

humble without being servile or scraping? (Page 83)

14. Are you experiencing the promises set forth on Pages 83 and 84?

ASSIGNMENT:

Note at this point the book assumes that you made a list of people you had harmed when you did your fourth Step inventory. If this has not been done, you should certainly make such a list at this point.

Next week discuss the balance of Chapter Six.

Week No. 15:

1. What are the specific instructions outlined for the taking of Step 10?
2. What do we watch for?
3. Note that "by this time sanity will have returned - we will seldom be interested in

    liquor." (Page 84) is this the sanity referred to in Step 2?

4. What is the proper use of will power? (Page 85)
5. What is the suggestion for taking the eleventh Step on a daily basis?
6. What do you watch for?
7. Do you practice this Step on a daily basis?
8. Do you follow the procedure outlined on Pages 86 and 87 regarding your daily morning meditations and the way you proceed through the day?
9. Has your attitude about a Power greater than yourself changed since you studied the chapter, "To the Agnostics"?
10. Do you believe "It Works -- It Really Does"? (Page 88)

ASSIGNMENT:
Read the chapter, "Working with Others".
Week No. 16:
Read and discuss the chapter, "Working with Others" at this meeting.

1. What are the step-by-step requirements for a twelfth Step?
2. Have you ever tried this? Share your experience with the group.

3. In cases where the alcoholic has not responded, have you worked with his/her family? Did you offer them your way of life, and what results did you have in this situation?
4. Do you believe that you should burn the idea into the consciousness of every man that he can get well regardless of anyone? The only condition is that he "trust in God and clean house."
5. Is this the basis of the statement that "this is a selfish program"? Is it really a selfish program in the true sense of those words?

Chapter Eight, "To the Wives", Chapter Nine, "The Family Afterward", Chapter Ten, "To Employers", and Chapter Eleven, "A Vision for You", are all chapters designed to teach you how to practice these principles in all your affairs. These chapters contain many spiritual truths which apply to all of us and should be read. Your group may decide whether or not you wish to discuss one or more of these chapters to conclude your Step Study.

A reading of the last portion of the book on Page 164 is a fitting way to end your Step study team. Haven't you really had the benefit of a contact with those who wrote this book. Don't you know now what you should really rely on?

ASSIGNMENT:

Find some new members of Alcoholics Anonymous who need this program and do another Step team study with them.

Printed in Great Britain
by Amazon

AA MEETINGS NORTH WEST WALES 2016

Day	Location	Time	Venue	Postcode
Monday	Llanrwst	20.00	Guide Hall, Llandogedd Rd (Nr R C Church)	LL26 0AU
Monday	Llangefni	19.30	St Josephs RC Church, Penmyndd Road	LL77 7HR
Monday	Bangor	20.00	Mind Centre, Abbey Road	LL57 2EA
Tuesday	Llangefni	11.00	St Josephs RC Church, Penmynydd Road	LL77 7HR
Tuesday	Porthmadog	19.30	Ebeneser Church (back of library) Chapel Street	LL49 9BT
Wednesday	Bangor	19.30	Mind Centre, Abbey Road	LL57 2EA
Thursday	Caernarfon	19.30	R C Church Hall, Eleanor Street, Twthill	LL55 1PF
Thursday	Holyhead	19.30	St Marys R C Church Hall, Longford Road	
Friday	Menai Bridge	noon	St Annes Church Hall, Dale Street	LL59 5AW
Friday	Bethesda	20.00	The Caban, Gerian (½ mile up from "Spa")	
Saturday	Caernarfon	19.30	R C Church Hall, Eleanor Street, Twthill	LL55 1PF
Sunday	Menai Bridge	18.30	St Annes Church Hall, Dale Street	LL59 5AH
Sunday	Dolgellau	10.30	Canteen, Farmers Mart, Bala Rd	LL40 2YF

ALANON

Day	Location	Time	Venue	Postcode
Friday	Menai Bridge	noon	St Annes Church Hall, Dale Street	LL59 5AH

ACCEPTANCE & DETACHMENT +
BIG PROBLEMS OUT OF LITTLE ONES
INTENTIONS ➔
SELF HONESTY
PATIENCE
TOLERANCE

GUILT / PRIDE
INADEQUACY
FEAR — FEAR
Remorse / By Honer
PERMIT THE ACTIONS OF
Others to deflect kindness